D0636222

Mitchell Symons was born in 1957 in London and educated at Mill House School and the LSE, where he studied law. Since leaving BBC TV, where he was a researcher and then a director, he has worked as a writer, broadcaster and journalist. He was a principal writer of early editions of the board game Trivial Pursuit and has devised many television formats. He is also the author of more than thirty books, and currently writes a weekly column for the *Sunday Express*.

www.rbooks.co.uk

Also by Mitchell Symons:

HOW TO AVOID A WOMBAT'S BUM

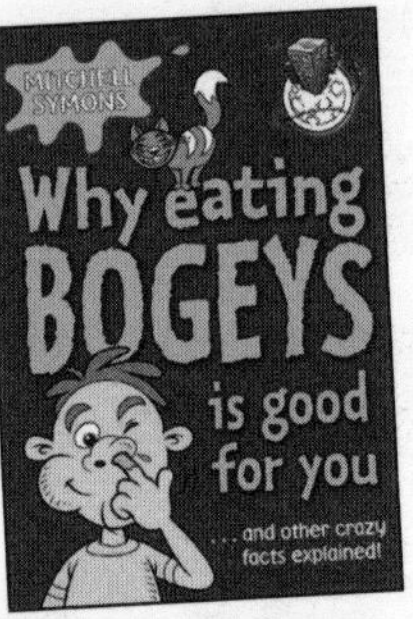

WHY EATING BOGEYS IS GOOD FOR YOU

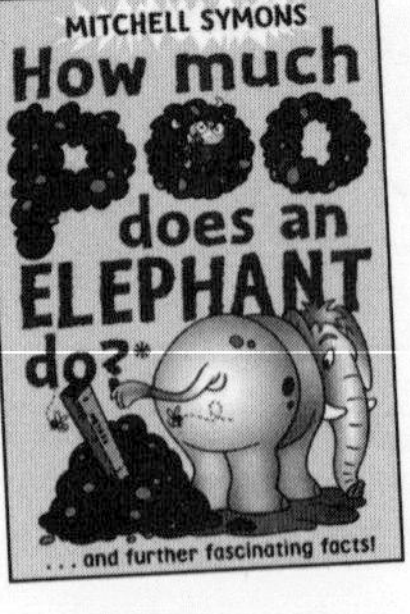

HOW MUCH POO DOES AN ELEPHANT DO?

MITCHELL SYMONS

Why do FARTS smell like rotten eggs?

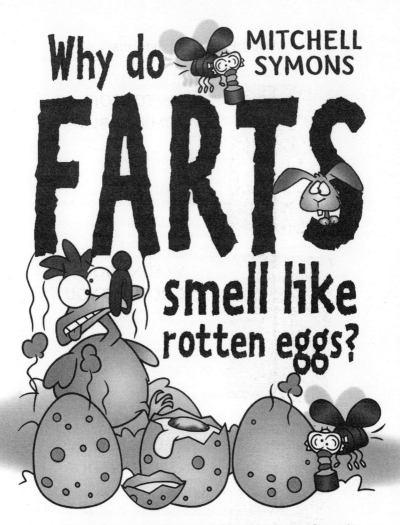

... and more crazy facts explained!

DOUBLEDAY

WHY DO FARTS SMELL LIKE ROTTEN EGGS?
A DOUBLEDAY BOOK 978 0 385 61561 7

Published in Great Britain by Doubleday,
an imprint of Random House Children's Books
A Random House Group Company

This edition published 2009

1 3 5 7 9 10 8 6 4 2

Text copyright © Mitchell Symons, 2009
Illustrations copyright © Artful Doodlers, 2009

The right of Mitchell Symons to be identified as the author of this work has been asserted in accordance with the Copyright, Designs and Patents Act 1988.

All rights reserved. No part of this publication may be reproduced, stored in a retrieval system, or transmitted in any form or by any means, electronic, mechanical, photocopying, recording or otherwise, without the prior permission of the publishers.

The Random House Group Limited supports the Forest Stewardship Council (FSC), the leading international forest certification organization. All our titles that are printed on Greenpeace-approved FSC-certified paper carry the FSC logo. Our paper procurement policy can be found at www.rbooks.co.uk/environment.

FSC Mixed Sources
Product group from well-managed forests and other controlled sources
www.fsc.org Cert no. TT-COC-2139
© 1996 Forest Stewardship Council

Set in Optima

RANDOM HOUSE CHILDREN'S BOOKS
61–63 Uxbridge Road, London W5 5SA

www.kidsatrandomhouse.co.uk
www.rbooks.co.uk

Addresses for companies within The Random House Group Limited can be found at: www.randomhouse.co.uk/offices.htm

THE RANDOM HOUSE GROUP Limited Reg. No. 954009

A CIP catalogue record for this book is available from the British Library.

Printed and bound in Great Britain by Clays Ltd, St Ives plc

To all of you who bought
the book because of the title,
and to all of you who bought
the book *despite* the title.

A couple of years ago I wrote a book – *Why Eating Bogeys Is Good For You** – not expecting very much to happen. And then, incredibly, it became a bestseller. The only explanation for its success that I can think of is that I wasn't trying to second-guess my readers: the questions were ones that I myself was really keen to know the answer to. Questions like: *Do identical twins have identical fingerprints? Do two wrongs make a right? Why is the sea blue? Is it cheaper to send yourself as a parcel to Australia rather than flying on an aeroplane?* and *Why did anyone even bother trying to put Humpty Dumpty back together again?*

There were more – many more: *Do you lose weight when you eat celery? Can you knock yourself out using just your own fist? What happens to a cow if you don't milk it? Why would anyone want to pop a weasel? What would happen to aeroplane passengers if someone opened the emergency exit while it was in the air?* and, yes, *Is eating bogeys bad for you?* (and I think we know the answer to that one!)

Sometimes, the best questions yielded the most disappointing answers; other times, it worked out exactly the other way round and a dumb question resulted in a fascinating answer. For me, it was just great fun finding out. So much so that I decided to tackle some more questions. Once again, I started with the questions that fascinated, me but now I had an advantage: after the publication of *Why Eating Bogeys Is Good For You*, I had a whole list of questions sent in by readers and quite a few from friends who'd (often in spite of themselves) found the book more than a little fascinating. Now I had something else to work with – something more than my own curiosity.

* It is – but only your own

So let me thank all the readers and friends who asked such extraordinary questions as: *Why does vomit always contain carrots? Has anyone ever been rescued after sending a message in a bottle? Why* shouldn't *you be able to have your cake and eat it?* And *Do lemmings really jump off cliffs? Who is the unluckiest person ever? Does eating jelly babies make you a cannibal? Why is wee-wee sometimes yellow and other times clear? Is there any penguin in a penguin biscuit?* (thanks for that one, Jonathan!) Once again, where possible, I went to experts for the answers. My thanks to them all. I also, of course, used my large library of reference books as well as the internet (although I tried to use this to check facts rather than, as is so tempting, as a tool of first resort).

Now for some even more important acknowledgements because without these people, this book couldn't have been written at all (in alphabetical order): Luigi Bonomi, Lauren Buckland, Penny Chorlton, Annie Eaton and Rhys Willson.

In addition, I'd also like to thank the following people for their help, contributions and/or support: Gilly Adams, Paul Donnelley, Jonathan Fingerhut, Jenny Garrison, Bryn Musson, Shannon Park, Nicholas Ridge, Mari Roberts Charlie Symons, Jack Symons, Louise Symons, David Thomas, Martin Townsend and Rob Woolley.

If I've missed anyone out, then please know that – as with any mistakes in the book – it is, as ever, entirely down to my own stupidity.

Mitchell Symons, 2009
thatbook@mail.com

Has anyone ever been rescued after sending a message in a bottle?

Picture a man on a desert island – yup, I'm also thinking of Robinson Crusoe. He's been stranded for some time when he finds a bottle. So he gets out his pen and a piece of paper (always assuming that he remembered to take them with him when he got shipwrecked) and writes a message which he puts into the bottle and chucks out to sea.

Several weeks later, someone picks up his message and sends out a ship to rescue him.

Surely that's the stuff of stories?

Well, it turns out that the scenario I've set out might have some truth to it.

For example, in May 2005 Costa Rican officials said 86 shipwrecked migrants had been rescued after fishermen found a message saying 'Please help us' in a bottle they had thrown overboard. The migrants, mainly teenagers from Ecuador and Peru, had been adrift in their packed boat for three days. The vessel had been floating near Cocos Island, a nature reserve over 350 miles off the Costa Rican coast. It's thought that the group was abandoned by people smugglers when the vessel got into trouble. The smugglers stripped the boat of radio and communication equipment when they left it. Without sending a message in a bottle, it's almost certain that they'd never have been rescued and would have all died.

In the course of my research, I found a fascinating twist on the message-in-a-bottle story. In January 2008, the chance discovery of a message in a bottle helped two lost climbers in Portland, Oregon, in the US to find their way off Mount Hood after a night spent huddled in a hastily built snow cave.

Instead of writing a message and putting it in a bottle, they came out of their cave to find a plastic bottle containing map coordinates giving their precise location, hanging on a twig with red tape on it.

Luckily for them, it turned out that the bottle had been hung on the tree by participants in a recent 'geocaching' contest (a sort of orienteering) in which people follow GPS coordinates to remote, far-flung locations.

The exhausted climbers spotted it just as searchers called their cell phones – which they mistakenly thought had stopped working the night before.

27-year-old Justin Votos and 28-year-old Matthew Pitts were able to tell the searchers (volunteers from Portland Mountain Rescue and the Air Force Reserve's 304th Rescue Squadron) precisely where they were, and were then talked down to safety.

So the moral to these stories is: 'Messages in bottles save lives'!

Why *shouldn't* you be able to have your cake and eat it?

Hear hear! After all, isn't that the whole point of cake – to eat it? So why then do people say 'You can't have your cake and eat it'?

The answer is that the expression itself is at fault! It should be 'You can't eat your cake

and still have it' – i.e. once you've eaten your cake, it will be gone – which is obviously true. In fact, put like this, you can see why a parent might say to a child who wants to spend all their pocket money and still have money to save, 'You can't have your cake and eat it.'

Even though it would confuse the child considerably . . .

So was there a McDonald who started McDonald's?

Yes and no. There was a McDonald – two of 'em as it happens – but they weren't responsible (in any meaningful sense) for the success of McDonald's.

The McDonald's legend began in 1954 with a man named Ray Kroc, who was working as a milkshake machine salesman. He visited Mac and Dick McDonald's smart hamburger restaurant in San Bernardino, California, to sell them some machines, and was so impressed with the quality of everything he saw, from the standard of hygiene to the quality of the food and the speed of the service, that he asked if they would allow him to open a 'copycat' branch under a franchise in Des Plaines, Illinois.

Most fast-food outlets at the time were rather seedy and a magnet for the new 'teenagers' and not the sort of places where families could take young children and elderly relatives out to eat.

In 1961, Ray Kroc, frustrated that the McDonald brothers didn't share his plans for expansion, bought all the rights to the McDonalds' operation for $2.7 million. Within a decade he had opened no fewer than 500 American branches. He also issued franchises but buyers were subjected to anonymous inspections to maintain uniform standards: the key to its success was that every aspect of production was tightly controlled. American staff were trained at the Hamburger University near Chicago. The grill men were taught to move from left to right, putting out six rows of burgers. They then had to flip the third row first, then the fourth, fifth and sixth, before the first and the second.

The golden arches were introduced in 1968, by which time global recognition was established. One potato in 12 grown in the US is bought by McDonald's for their fries and the operation is by far the biggest consumer of beef, despite the existence of many other fast-food chains.

Today, McDonald's is the number one fast-food empire in the world, with more than 1,400 restaurants in about 70 countries, and the gigantic golden arches symbol is probably the most recognized brand in the world after Coca-Cola.

38 million people a day eat a McDonald's meal – equivalent to the entire population of Spain, including the Canaries!

Indeed, if all the hamburgers produced by McDonald's in a year were laid in a straight line, they would stretch five times round the world or would reach nearly 2,000 times higher than Mount Everest.

How come spiders don't get caught in their own webs?

Fortunately for spiders (though not their victims), their legs are coated in a natural oil that stops them getting trapped in their own webs.

Is it true that the Romans ate so much that they had special places – vomitoriums – where they could be sick during and after meals?

No, it isn't. While it's absolutely true that the Romans gorged themselves stupid, especially during banquets and feasts, they didn't have a special place to throw up: they just did it when and where they liked.

The reason why people get confused over this question is because of the 'vomitorium'. They assume that because Romans threw up a lot as a result of over-indulgence and had vomitoriums (or 'vomitoria'), then that's where they did their puking.

But no! In fact vomitoriums were passageways and tunnels in the great amphitheatres like the Coliseum: they were there to make sure that people weren't crushed on their way in or out.

And these were called vomitoriums because people were spewed out of the amphitheatres extraordinarily quickly.

Why do we sweat?

Our bodies work best when we are about 98.6°F (37°C). Thanks to the ability to sweat, our bodies stay cool – otherwise we wouldn't be able to tolerate heat and our bodies would eventually explode from over-heating.

When your body gets too hot – for example, after exercise, or because you are dressed too warmly for the weather or the central heating is too high – you start to feel uncomfortable.

Your brain can deal with this problem very quickly by using the part of it that controls temperature, which is called the *hypothalamus*, and it sends an urgent message to your body, telling it to sweat. The sweat glands – of which there are millions all over our bodies – start making sweat (also known as perspiration), which leaves your skin through tiny holes called pores. Sweat is made almost completely of water, salt and sugar. When the sweat hits the air, the air makes it evaporate (this means it turns from a liquid to a vapour). As the sweat evaporates off your skin, you cool down.

Sweat is a great cooling system, but if you're sweating a lot on a hot day or after playing hard you could be losing too much water through your skin. Then you need to put liquid back in your body by drinking plenty of water so you don't get dehydrated.

Sweat by itself doesn't smell at all. It's the bacteria that live on your skin that mix with the sweat and give it a stinky smell. So it's stale sweat – rather than sweat itself – that smells. And sweaty unwashed clothes can really honk! Fortunately, regular washing with soap and water keeps most of us fresh and nice to be near. However, when you reach puberty, special hormones affect the glands in your armpits, and these glands make some individuals smellier than others: these people may need a gentle hint to wash more, or use products that will help them become nicer to be around.

All of which begs the question: do other mammals sweat?

To which the answer is: some do, some don't.

Dogs, for example, don't have sweat glands so if they overheat, they either seek shade,

or pant heavily and lose heat through their tongues. This is why it's so very dangerous to leave dogs to overheat in cars as their cooling mechanism isn't as good as ours.

Horses, on the other hand, do sweat, but because they're covered in so much hair, their sweat doesn't evaporate so easily and therefore they have to be cooled down (e.g. with a towel) or else they can get very ill.

But what about the pig? After all, we talk about sweating like a pig – so presumably the pig sweats a lot?

In fact, pigs don't sweat. What they do to cool down is either drink lots of water or find a nice mud bath or wet patch and roll in it! The mud also helps keep flies and mosquitoes away, so pigs are quite clever – very clever in fact: the mud also acts as a sunscreen and the pink ones would otherwise get pretty sunburned on hot days as they are not very hairy either. So although they often look dirty, there is a good reason for this, and contrary to what most people think, they are in fact quite fastidious and only smelly if their owners don't clean them out regularly. Think about it: if you had to live in a space with all your wee and poo, how pleasant would *you* smell? Given a choice of fresh dry bedding and stinky smelly wet bedding, any pig will always choose the former. And the fact that they eat leftovers and other stuff considered unfit for humans is again not their choice . . . I'm quite sure that if you offered the average pig the choice of a clean bucket of fresh wholesome food or a bucket of pungent semi-rotting stuff, his snout would be in the former first rather than the latter. So next time you hear someone use the expression 'dirty pig', you can correct them.

Is it known who designed the map of the London Underground?

Yes, it is. It was a man named Harry Beck in 1933 and his design is still the basis of the map we use today, which is justifiably regarded as the most brilliant example of its kind. Incredibly, he was paid just five guineas (£5.25) for his work.

Incidentally, while we're on the subject of the London Underground, only one person was ever born in a tube carriage. Thelma Ursula Beatrice Eleanor (check out her initials) was born in 1924 on a Bakerloo line train at Elephant & Castle.

Why can we blow bubbles with bubble gum but not with chewing gum?

Bubble gum is made with five main ingredients: chewing-gum base, sugar, softeners, flavourings and colours. It's the gum base that gives the 'chew' and the 'bubble', but it's rosin, a product of trees, that enhances the texture of the gum base to make it better for blowing bubbles – along with softeners – made with refined vegetable oil products – to keep the gum soft.

The Greeks were chewing a type of gum as early as the year AD 50, but the first bubble gum wasn't invented until 1906, when a man named Frank H. Fleer made a gum he called Blibber-Blubber, a silly name for a too-sticky gum. It didn't sell because the only way to get a popped bubble off your skin was to scrub it with turpentine.

Twenty years later, in 1928, a less sticky bubble gum called Dubble Bubble was invented by Walter Diemer, a 23-year-old who worked as an accountant for the Fleer Chewing Gum Company in Philadelphia. In his spare time he experimented with new gum recipes. One was different from the others – it was stretchier and less sticky than regular chewing gum. While making the first batch of what was to become Dubble Bubble, he added pink colouring to make the gum look more appealing. It happened to be the only food colouring he had to hand . . .

With the approval of his boss, he offered a five-pound lump of the stuff to a grocery store. It sold out in a single afternoon. Needless to say, before long Fleer were selling Diemer's bubble gum and Diemer himself was teaching cheeky salesmen to blow bubbles, to demonstrate exactly what made this gum different from all other gums.

Dubble Bubble remained unchallenged for years – at least until Bazooka came along in the 1940s. Bazooka was named after the humorous musical instrument which entertainer Bob Burns had fashioned from two gas pipes and a funnel in the 1930s. (This contraption also gave its name to the armour-piercing weapon developed during the Second World War).

Walter Diemer stayed with Fleer for decades, eventually becoming a senior vice president. He never received any royalties for his invention, but he didn't seem to mind. Sometimes he'd invite a group of kids to his house, where he enjoyed telling them the story of his wonderful, accidental invention. Then he'd hold bubble-blowing contests for them. He died in 1998 at the age of 94.

Wrigley's, the world's largest gum manufacturer, started making Hubba Bubba bubble gum in the 1970s. Like all modern bubble gums, this doesn't stick to your face when you blow bubbles and they explode!

Why is flu called flu?

No, it's got nothing to do with the fact that the disease 'flew' around (besides the fact that it is, of course, spelled differently).

In fact, flu is short for 'influenza', and that got its name from the fact that people believed that flu epidemics were due to the evil 'influence' of certain stars in the sky.

Why 'as happy as a clam' – why not some other shellfish?

It's important to know the rest of this saying. It should be 'As happy as a clam at high tide'. Why? Because clams are only harvested when the tide is out, so when it's high-tide, they're safe – and therefore happy!

Is it dangerous to pick a scab?

The skin has a wonderful way of healing itself – if you let it. Whenever you damage your skin, special blood cells called platelets are released to repair the damage.

These platelets rapidly stick together like glue at the cut, forming a clot. The clot forms a safe and protective 'plaster' made of human tissue over the wound and stops more blood and other fluids leaking out. The clot uses other blood cells and thread-like stuff called fibrin to help hold the clot together.

Left alone, the clot gradually hardens and then dries out to form a scab, which is usually crusty and dark red or brown. The scab protects the wound by keeping germs out while the skin underneath gets busy re-growing. As well as new skin cells, any damaged blood vessels are also being fixed. White blood cells, the ones that help fight other infections, zoom in to attack any germs that might have sneaked into the wound, especially in mud or dirt or contaminated water. These white blood cells also get rid of any dead blood and skin cells that may still be hanging around the cut.

Eventually, if you leave it alone to get on with it (usually after at least a week but maybe longer if it is bigger and thicker), the scab falls off and underneath – hey presto! – there is brand new skin. However, if you pick the scab (and yes, I know it's unbelievably tempting), you can undo the repair and rip your skin again: it'll probably take longer to heal – worse if your fingers are dirty, or you expose the wound to further bugs, it can get infected.

If you keep picking at it (now *don't*), you may even get a scar. So tempting though it is to pick away (*stop it!*), it really is best to leave well alone and allow your body to heal itself: let the scab come away when it's ready to.

Why is a pack of cards divided into clubs, diamonds, hearts and spades?

This comes from the Middle Ages when playing cards first became (relatively) common. The four suits (as clubs, diamonds, hearts and spades are known) represented the four most important parts of society in the Middle Ages.

So clubs represented agriculture,
diamonds represented the merchant class,
hearts represented the church
and spades represented the military.

Incidentally, the reason I list the suits in that

order (clubs, diamonds, hearts and spades) is because that is their (ascending) order in the game of bridge – the most fascinating and intelligent card game in the world.

Which came first – Coca-Cola or Pepsi-Cola?

In 1886, in Atlanta, Georgia, in the United States, a pharmacist named Dr John Stith Pemberton was trying to find a headache cure when he came up with his recipe for Coca-Cola. Pemberton was excited by reports of the virtues of the coca plant, which had been chewed by the natives of Peru and Bolivia for over 2,000 years. It was reputed to act as a stimulant, aid to digestion and life-extender. Although he had invented numerous patent medicines, his ambition as he turned 50 was to find a drink that could earn him a place in history. He decided to base his new drink around this plant. He made up the Coca-Cola syrup in (according to legend) a three-legged brass pot in his back yard. The new drink, made fizzy by carbonated water, was sold for five cents a glass.

Dr Pemberton always kept his recipe a secret and the Coca-Cola company has zealously guarded it ever since by keeping it in a vault – even refusing to supply countries which insist on knowing the precise contents.* The formula is sent in a concentrate to bottling factories all over the world, where it is made with purified local water.

Coca-Cola remained basically a soda fountain drink until nationwide bottling started in 1899. The distinctive, classic Coca-Cola bottle was launched in 1916 after a national competition: the winning design by Earl R. Dean of the Roof Glass Company of Terre Haute, Indiana, drew inspiration from a coca pod.

As for the name of the drink, that was down to Frank M. Robinson, Dr Pemberton's partner and book-keeper, who suggested 'Coca-Cola'. He then wrote it in his inimitable handwriting, thereby instantly creating the logo that is now recognized by 94% of the world's population.

Alas, neither Pemberton nor Robinson benefited much from their creation, which is now the world's number one brand. It is sold in over 195 countries – 705 million servings every day – or 13,000 servings every second – to an incredible six billion customers.

Meanwhile, in 1893, seven years after Dr Pemberton invented Coca-Cola, another American named Caleb Bradham came up with what would become Pepsi-Cola.

Bradham owned a drug store in New Bern, North Carolina, which, like most drug stores of its day, had a soda fountain. Bradham decided to create his own soda – a blend of cola nut extract, vanilla and 'rare oils' that he originally called 'Brad's Drink'.

After a few years of selling his drink under this name, he decided on a new name – calling it Pepsi-Cola after a combination of the words 'pepsin' and 'cola' as he believed that his drink aided digestion much like the pepsin enzyme did (even though it was not used as an ingredient), and would help people with 'peptic' ulcers.

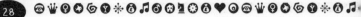

Bradham realized that if he bottled his recipe he could distribute it beyond North Carolina and so he copied Coca-Cola's example and set up bottling franchises to anyone who wanted them. By the First World War, he had more than 300 bottlers signed up. Sugar was rationed in the war and this severely reduced production, so Bradham decided to stockpile vast amounts of it. Unfortunately for him, in 1923 the price of sugar plummeted and he was forced to sell his company. He even offered it to Coca-Cola but they didn't want it. Pepsi was on the point of disappearing altogether but in 1931 was bought by the Loft Candy Company, which owned a chain of sweet shops. Despite the Depression that followed, Pepsi survived. The new owners doubled the size of the bottles without raising the five cent price. Pepsi became the drink anyone could afford, being half the price of Coca-Cola.

*In a 1993 book, *For God, Country and Coca-Cola,* author Mark Pendergrast 'revealed' the recipe. Apparently, the ingredients include: water, lime juice, sugar, citric acid, citrate caffeine, vanilla extract, caramel and the following flavourings: oil of orange, lemon, cinnamon, nutmeg, coriander and neroli.

Why is a hamburger called a hamburger when it's made from beef and not from ham?

That's because it's *not* named after ham but after the German city of Hamburg where the hamburger was first eaten.

In fact, it wasn't the beef patty that we know as a hamburger but a flat German sausage that was squeezed between two pieces of bread for eating when on the move. When Germans emigrated to America in the 1880s, they took their meat snack with them. The word 'hamburger' was coined when a Washington newspaper used it to describe the meal eaten by thousands of people at the St Louis World's Fair in 1904. Later, the hamburger became popular in factories because, like the sandwich or the pasty, it was something that workers could eat without stopping to find a knife and fork and a plate.

However, the confusion over the 'ham' in hamburger persists to this day, many restaurants and shops get round the problem by calling it a beefburger.

What's the origin of the expression 'It's all fun and games until someone loses an eye'?

This is something my mother used to say to me and my friends when we were playing a bit too roughly. As I recall – although it is a very long time ago (I am very old indeed) – the dialogue went something like this.

Setting: the garden of my childhood house.

MITCH'S MUM: I think you'd better calm down, lads.

MITCH & HIS FRIENDS (*briefly stop screaming, laughing and beating each other up*): We're only having fun!

MITCH'S MUM: Well, it's all fun and games until someone loses an eye.

She departs and Mitch and his friends go back to what they were doing.

I thought that she was just being literal – and maybe she was! But in fact this derives from Ancient Rome, where during wrestling matches there was just one rule: no eye-gouging. So if one of the wrestlers poked someone's eye out, then all the fun and games would indeed be over!

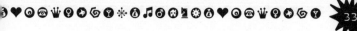

Why do we call someone who's putting forward an opposing point of view a 'devil's advocate'?

Sometimes, during a discussion or debate, someone will say, 'Hang on a minute, let me play devil's advocate here,' and then go on to put forward an entirely different point of view – not necessarily one that he or she believes in – so that both sides of the debate can be considered.

The idea of the devil's advocate comes from the Roman Catholic church. When they're deciding if a person should be made a saint, a devil's advocate – called just that – is appointed to give an alternative view.

Why do we blow on a hot drink to cool it down but blow on our hands to warm them up?

This sounds incredibly contradictory, doesn't it? But really it's quite simple. Let's agree that your breath is a constant 37°C, OK? The hot drink is, say, 80°C – therefore your breath is cooler and cools it down.

Now let's take your hands. On a cold day, they might be 10°C. Your breath is still 37°C so it's hotter and therefore warms them.

Same action – different effect!

Does sugar make children hyperactive?

No, it doesn't – despite what your parents might think! Dr Kleinman is Professor of Pediatrics (children's medicine) at the Harvard Medical School in Boston and so he knows a little more about the subject than your mum and dad do! He says, 'There are no studies to show that sugar in the commonly eaten foods makes children overly active or causes them to be hyperactive and have attention deficit.'

Interestingly, the reason why parents believe that it does is because the times when they see their children getting hyperactive and over-excited tend to coincide with the times when they're allowed to eat lots of sugar – at events like children's birthday parties. But it's the occasion rather than the sugar that makes them so fizzy.

Having said that, if the children are taking in lots of artificial colours (E numbers) as well as sugar, then this could equally explain over-excitable behaviour.

Why is a sidekick so called?

There's a difference of opinion in my house over this one! My wife has looked into this and reckons that it comes from slang used by pickpocketers – something to do with the front side-pocket of a pair of trousers being known as a 'kick'. Because this was the pocket that was least likely to be 'picked', the 'side kick' became slang for your best friend or companion.

No, I didn't think so either. So I did my own research and discovered that in America's Wild West of the late 19th century, friends you rode with were known as side-pals and side-partners – because they rode at your side. Sometimes they were also called side-kickers because, in the language of the time, you kicked along together.

This got shortened to side-kicks and, over time, the hyphen was lost – as is so often the case with terms and words that get used a lot – and it became 'sidekicks'.

I'm sure I'm right, but then my wife is sure she is.

You'll have to decide for yourself!

Are black and white colours?

Black definitely isn't. In fact, it's the total absence of colour. Black absorbs all colours in the spectrum and blocks them.

It's harder to say with white: as it blends all the colours in the spectrum and reflects them back as white. So, in a sense, it's an amalgamation of colours as well as itself.

Incidentally, this explains why snow is white even though the water that makes up the snow is itself transparent.

What is a red herring?

A red herring is an irrelevance – something that distracts attention from important things.

But why should a herring be used to describe such a thing? And why red?

In the 19th century, a red herring was another name for the smoked herring or kipper.

During a hunt, if someone wanted to distract the hounds from following the scent of an animal, then they would put down a kipper (or red herring) and this would work extremely well.

In fact, huntsmen themselves, when training their hounds, would use red herrings so that the dogs would learn to ignore the stronger smell and continue to follow the weaker scent of a fox or a badger.

From there, it isn't hard to see why the expression was used to describe the laying of false clues in detective novels.

Why do people say 'For Pete's sake'?

This is an old-fashioned expression – expressing annoyance and/or exasperation – but you still hear people using it.

It goes back to the days when, for religious reasons, people were reluctant to say 'For God's sake' or 'For Christ's sake'.

But why, you might wonder, Pete? It doesn't even sound like God or Christ.

The answer is simple: Pete was St Peter, the apostle who became the very first leader of the Christian religion.

Was there a real James Bond?

Sort of. Ian Fleming, the creator of Bond, worked in Naval Intelligence during the Second World War and met many men on whom he could have based his character (and it's interesting to note that Commander Bond did, of course, have a naval background).

However, there are two men who really inspired the great action hero: the first was Patrick Dalzel-Job, a naval officer who led wartime missions in Norway before serving with Fleming in France and Germany as part of an undercover assault unit, which travelled ahead of the Allied advance and seized German equipment and documents before they could be destroyed. The second man was Fleming's elder brother, Peter, who also served with distinction on missions in Norway, Greece and South-East Asia. Add Ian Fleming's own experiences and a bit of imagination and then you have the recipe for James Bond.

The name of James Bond was based on a real person – not a spy but an ornithologist. Fleming was a keen birdwatcher, and when he was looking for a name, he picked up a book by a distinguished American ornithologist called James Bond and decided to 'borrow' the name.

By the way, if you fancy showing off, just ask your mum or dad who the first James Bond was. They're bound to say Sean Connery, who was indeed the first actor to play him in a film (*Dr No*), but the correct answer is Barry Nelson who, in 1954, played James Bond in a one-hour US TV version of *Casino Royale*.

Given that we now have equality of the sexes, is it still 'Women and children first' in the lifeboats?

Last year we went on a cruise and, as usual, they kicked off with the lifeboat drill. Having been on a fair few cruises, I ignored most of what was being said until I heard the captain announce that, 'In the unlikely event of the ship having to be evacuated, passengers would be helped into the lifeboats, children and women first . . .'

'Hang on,' I said to the first officer I came across. 'That's not right. Women have fought damn hard for equality – and they thoroughly deserve it. So why doesn't that extend to being treated equally when it comes to ships sinking?' The officer smiled and shrugged his shoulders but I wasn't mollified, and after the cruise I phoned other cruise companies. In theory, I was told, people board lifeboats with their partners and families – irrespective of gender – but, in an emergency the rule of 'women and children first' would still prevail. However all the companies assured me that 'there are spaces in the lifeboats for everyone'.

Given that Teflon is meant to be a non-stick substance, how does it stick to the frying pan to make it a non-stick pan?

In fact, it's quite simple. Teflon (or PolyTetraFluoroEthylene, a fluorocarbon

plastic and reputedly the most inert substance known to man) is applied in layers. The first layer is a primer designed to stick to the metal surface of the pan. Then – and only then – are the non-stick layers applied on top.

Was there ever a Granny Smith?

Yes, there was. The original Granny Smith was Maria Smith (ne Sherwood), who emigrated from Britain to Australia in 1838 with her husband Thomas and their five surviving children, and established a successful fruit farm in New South Wales. In 1868, she discovered a seedling apple growing on her farm that had developed from the remains of some French crab apples from Tasmania. The resulting mutation became the apple that would immortalize her – although Maria, who died in 1870, didn't live to enjoy her success. The Granny Smith was introduced into the UK in the 1930s and has been popular ever since.

Has anyone ever 'broken the bank' at a casino?

Let me tell you – warn you – that, when it comes to gambling in a casino, there's only one winner: the casino.

Having said that, there is the story – and song – of 'The Man Who Broke the Bank at Monte Carlo'. Incredibly, it is (sort of) true!

In 1873, Joseph Jagger, a mechanic and engineer who worked in Yorkshire cotton mills, visited the Casino Beaux-Arts in Monte Carlo. He soon realized that the roulette wheels couldn't produce truly random numbers as each wheel would have a different balance. This meant that there would be a bias in favour of certain numbers. So he hired a team of clerks to record every number that came up and discovered that one of the casino's wheels produced nine numbers far more frequently than the laws of probability would suggest. Jagger then embarked on stage two of his operation. He sat at the 'inaccurate' wheel and placed bets on the nine numbers in question. Within four days he had won over a million French francs. The casino, however, fought back and moved their roulette wheels around. Jagger went to his usual table and lost heavily before realizing (because of a minuscule scratch on 'his' wheel) what had happened. There then ensued a cat-and-mouse game between him and the casino, but by the end he'd still managed to amass a profit in excess of two

million francs (about £600,000 in today's money). The casino was obliged to close down while they rebuilt their roulette wheels to ensure that Jagger's feat could never be repeated, so in the sense that he stopped them trading, Jagger could be said to have 'broken' them. He left Monte Carlo and never returned. After his death in 1892, Fred Gilbert immortalized him in the song, 'The Man Who Broke the Bank at Monte Carlo'.

Do lemmings really jump off cliffs?

I'd always heard that this was a myth perpetuated by a TV documentary but, hey, what do I know? So I phoned my pal Lucy, who used to work at the Natural History Museum, and she told me that lemmings *don't* jump off cliffs. 'There's an element of truth in it but only a tiny bit. The Norwegian lemming does migrate a small distance during spring and autumn in search of food and, very occasionally, if food really can't be found, they will travel great distances in huge numbers. This can lead to deaths along the way – especially when they're crossing water – but that doesn't mean that they're dying intentionally. Think of a football crowd surging forward – well, that's what happens on these mass migrations.'

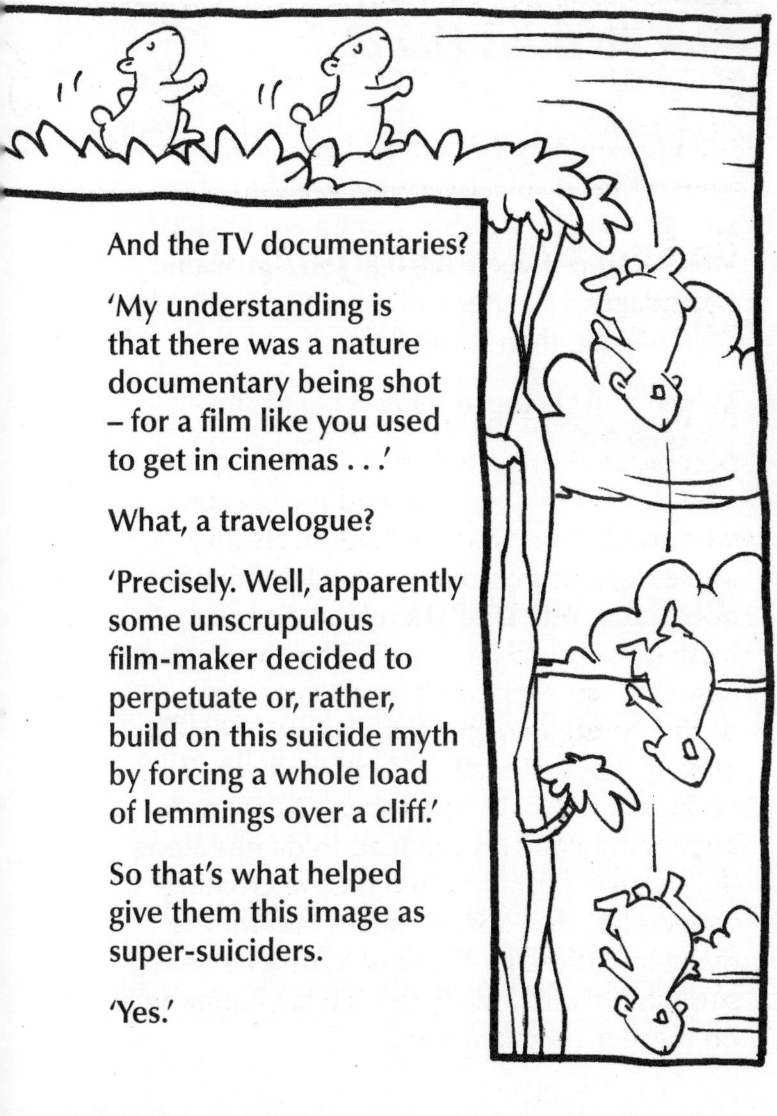

And the TV documentaries?

'My understanding is that there was a nature documentary being shot – for a film like you used to get in cinemas . . .'

What, a travelogue?

'Precisely. Well, apparently some unscrupulous film-maker decided to perpetuate or, rather, build on this suicide myth by forcing a whole load of lemmings over a cliff.'

So that's what helped give them this image as super-suiciders.

'Yes.'

How do ships float?

Things – objects, people and, yes, ships – float if they displace more water than they weigh. So even if a ship – say, a cruise ship – weighs more than a 100,000 tons, provided it displaces a greater weight of water than its own weight, then it will float.

Which must come as a big relief to the passengers!

Why do we burp?

When we eat or drink, we don't just swallow food or liquid, we also swallow air at the same time. The air we breathe contains gases and sometimes when you swallow these gases, they need to get out. That's where burping comes in! Extra gas is forced out of the stomach, up through the oesophagus (the tube for food that connects the back of the throat to the stomach), and then emerges from the mouth as a burp.

Obviously, there are some foods or drinks that cause us to burp more than others. For example, gaseous foods like onions or fizzy drinks can cause you to burp. Similarly, eating or drinking too fast can make a person burp because this can send extra air into the stomach. The same thing can happen when you drink through a straw as extra air gets taken in.

When you were very young, burping was considered a good thing and you were praised for doing it: when babies burp it means they have got rid of any extra gas in their stomachs that will be painful and make them cry (trust me: parents are delighted by *anything* that stops a baby crying).

However, as we get older, burping – especially loudly and in a prolonged manner – is considered to be ill-mannered.

I understand that, of course, and take great care not to burp in public, but sometimes you really can't help yourself and – oh well, it's better out than in, isn't it?

Well, that's my excuse anyway.

Is it true that cows lie down before it rains?

The sight of cows lying down in a field is enough to persuade some people that rain is coming very soon.

Are they right?

Sorry to disappoint you but I can't really give a conclusive answer.

Against the theory you could say that often half the cows in the field are standing up while the rest are lying down! And then there are some that are just lying down to have a good old chew rather than preparing for rain.

On the other hand, it is possible for cows (as it is for us) to sense dampness in the air and make sure they have somewhere dry to lie – especially if they fancied doing so anyway! Rather as we rush to get the washing in when it looks as if it might rain.

It's also important to note that animals can definitely sense changes in the weather before humans, especially in the case of really bad weather. Very few animals who were free to run actually drowned in the 2004 Asian tsunami. Keepers at the Yala National Park in Sri Lanka said that many species like elephants and leopards became restless several hours before the wave hit and started moving inland towards higher ground.

Did a sixth sense warn them of impending disaster? It is well-known that, except for eyesight, animal senses are far more sensitive than human ones simply because they have to depend on them for survival. Scientists theorize that the underwater earthquake that caused the tsunami produced vibrations and rumbling sounds beyond our human ability to detect; wildlife probably picked up these unusual signals and saved their lives by instinctively moving away from the source of danger. They may have also noticed changes in air pressure caused by the approaching surge.

So, on balance, I'd say that if you see a whole herd of cows lying down, then you should reckon on a shower at the very least.

Who is the unluckiest person ever?

Oh gosh, there are so many candidates for such an appalling position, but a man named Frank Perkins of Los Angeles in the US might just be the 'winner'.

In 1992, poor Mr Perkins made an attempt on the world flagpole-sitting record. Suffering from flu, he came down eight hours short of the 400-day record.

Just to make matters even worse for the

hapless Perkins, he then discovered that his sponsor had gone bust, his girlfriend had left him and his phone and electricity had been cut off.

You have to admit that's pretty unlucky.

Is the glass half empty or half full?

At the moment, it's half empty – but then the sun's just gone in and I can't find any chocolate in the house. Yesterday was a good day and so it was half full. But what do I know? Fortunately, my friend Stuart has a degree in philosophy and was therefore able to offer a more objective approach. 'OK, let's look at it this way. This is a metaphor for whether you're an optimist or a pessimist. It's as simple as that. From a purely practical point of view, however, I'd say that if you have a full pint of beer and you drink half of it, then it is half empty. On the other hand, if you take an empty pint glass to the bar and ask for a half-pint, then the glass will become half full. All right? Good, then it's your round. And mine's a pint.'

Why is it considered bad luck to say 'Macbeth' in a theatre?

We've all heard actors referring to 'the Scottish Play' rather than dare to utter the 'M' word, but why? I phoned my old friend Barry, who's an actor – in as much as that's the profession he puts on his passport (he's unemployed for fifty weeks of the year and

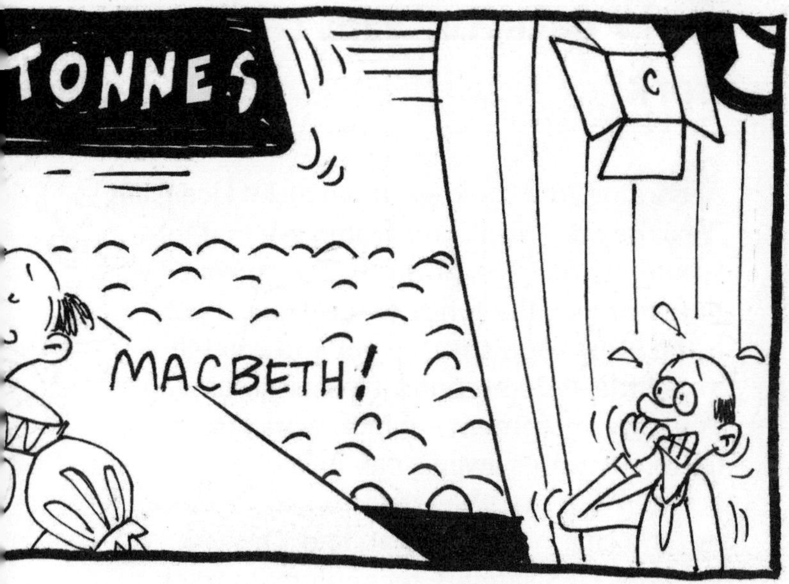

then earns enough from a couple of cheesy telly ads to make up for it).

He told me, 'There was a time – happy days – when every town had its own theatre. If a play wasn't doing well, the theatre would take it off and put on an old crowd-pleaser like *Macbeth*. From this grew the idea that *Macbeth* was unlucky because it was only used when another play had bombed.'

Do TV detector vans really work?

According to a spokeswoman at TV Licensing, 'Yes, they do.' Well, you *would* say that, wouldn't you? 'No, honestly, the current TV detector van, the tenth model since 1952, is the most sophisticated yet and can tell in as little as 20 seconds if a TV is in use. The new equipment – which works from up to 60 metres away – can pinpoint the actual room that the television set is in but not the channel being watched. Detector vans use GPS satellite technology to track

down specific addresses to precisely target individual suspected evader-homes, using up-to-the-minute information from its database of 28 million addresses. 7,500 components have been used to make up the ground-breaking technology in the new vans, which were developed in such secrecy that engineers working on specific detection methods worked in isolation.

'The new vans are the first to be designed with removable TV Licensing branding. This makes them look like any other white van on the streets.'

What's the difference between an assassination and a murder?

I ran this past my pet linguist, who told me, 'Both involve the premeditated taking of human life but while all assassinations are murders, not all murders are assassinations.

The key difference is that the target of an assassin is someone in public life – usually, though not necessarily, a politician. The victim is almost certainly not known personally by the assassin, who is therefore killing for money or for a cause, however misguided.

Did Neil Armstrong really walk on the moon or was the whole thing one huge hoax?

Conspiracy theorists are to the internet what fleas are to a dead fox: all over it. You can find a rebuttal of almost anything you ever thought true. The belief that the moon landings were all a hoax to get one over on the Russians would be laughable if it weren't trotted out so often. So let me dispel it merely by demonstrating that not only has no astronaut – former or present – confirmed any of the hoax theories but neither has any NASA scientist. So there you have it: on one side, the world of space travel; on the other, the sort of people who spend their nights alone in front of their computer screens. I know which side I believe . . .

Is it true that the first person to stop clapping at a Stalin rally was taken away to be shot?

Josef Stalin was the leader of communist Russia until his death in 1953. Like his enemy, Adolf Hitler, he exercised total power and so was really a dictator.

As such, he inspired huge fear among the people, and this explains why the standing

ovations at his rallies routinely lasted for an hour or longer. But is it true that the first person to stop clapping was taken away to be shot? 'Almost certainly not,' according to the historian I consulted. 'However, the fact is many people *thought* that that might happen – and, let's face it, Stalin was entirely capable of doing that – and therefore the standing ovations became an ordeal – even for Stalin himself. So, to stop them without any individual having to take responsibility for being the first, he used a bell to signal that the applause should stop.'

What's the difference between a hymn and a carol?

A hymn is specifically a song of praise to God (or to a saint, etc.) whereas a carol is any (almost always) celebratory song (almost always) connected with Christmas or, to a lesser extent, Easter. Originally, the carol was a communal dance of celebration, but when words were added to the tune, the resulting song became known as a carol.

Why do we talk about 'knuckling down' to do some task?

This comes from the game of marbles, where players would literally put their knuckles to the ground in order to take their best shots.

Why is the word 'toerag' used as an insult?

When they couldn't afford socks, tramps used to wrap pieces of cloth around their feet. These were known as 'toerags' and the word itself came to be applied to the people wearing them. From there, it went into the general language so that any 'inferior' person would be described in that way.

Why do well-wishers tell actors to 'break a leg'?

You can see why superstitious actors wouldn't want people to say 'good luck' as it's tempting fate. But why invite them to break their legs? There's a two-fold explanation: firstly, it's a form of reverse superstition (i.e. if good luck is tempting fate then wish them bad luck), and secondly,

it's a subtle way of saying that you hope the actor will be down on one knee at the end of the performance, bowing down before an appreciative audience – and, in olden days, picking up tips thrown on to the stage by grateful spectators.

Is every fourth year always a leap year?

Not quite. Let me explain.

Generally speaking, 29 February occurs once every four years because there aren't precisely 365 days in a year but approximately 365 and a quarter. That's to say it takes the earth 365¼ days to go round the sun and complete an astronomical year.

This extra day every four years allows the man-made calendar to catch up with the astronomical calendar.

So far, so easy.

However, because it isn't *quite* a quarter day that needs to be added, we only need leap days 97 years (and not 100) out of 400. It is for this reason that we have this formula: there's a leap year every year that's divisible by four *unless* that year is divisible by 100. If it is divisible by 100, it would only be a leap year if that year was also divisible by 400 (as 2000 was). So although 1900 was divisible by four, it wasn't a leap year – even though 1896, four years earlier, had been.

Why isn't Mother's Day always on – or around – the same day every year?

In 2008, Mother's Day fell on 2 March, which was extremely early; sometimes it's as late as April. Why the inconsistency? Why not have it – say – on the first Sunday in March *every* year?

The reason for this is because Mother's Day – a day honouring mums – is always held on the same day as Mothering Sunday, which is when, historically, Christians returned home to their 'mother church'.

Since this was done on the fourth Sunday in Lent – or three weeks before Easter Sunday – Mother's Day follows the same pattern.

In other countries, where Mother's Day is NOT linked to Mothering Sunday, the date is often fixed. For example, in the US (and many other countries) it's always the second Sunday in May.

How did the game of poker get its name?

Poker is believed to have its origins in 11th century China. The earliest recorded mention of it in the west was in Louisiana in the early 19th century. In 1834, it was being played on the Mississippi riverboats, where it was known as the 'cheating game'. Within a few years it had acquired the name poker – even though it wasn't quite the game we know today (it was played with 20 cards instead of 52). Poker derives its name either from the 18th century French game 'poque' or the German game 'pochspiel'. There are, however, other possible derivations – the best of which is that it came from the slang word 'poke', meaning money: pickpockets used to relieve victims of their 'poke'.

Why is 666 'the mark of the beast'?

According to my pet theologian, it all started with the New Testament of the Bible. 'In the Book of Revelations (chapter 13, verse 18) it says, 'If anyone has insight, let him calculate the number of the beast for it is the man's number. His number is 666.' But you have to see it in the context of what was going on when it was written: when Jews and Christians were being persecuted for their faith by the Romans. They needed to warn each other but couldn't take the risk of using names and so used as numbers as code instead. Taking the name Nero, the most evil of all the Roman emperors, and adding an N – he was known as Neron in Hebrew – it translates as 666.' How? N equals 50, E is 6, R is 500, O is 60. From here, it was a short leap for the beast to become the devil.' The other, chilling, proof for the potency of 666 comes if you give A the value of 100, B the value of 101, C 102 and D 103, etc., the name Hitler scores 666.

Why are enthusiasts called 'buffs'?

As you know, anyone who's an expert on – or an enthusiast for – something (maybe films or stamps) is described as a buff. But what's the derivation? It turns out that in 19th-century New York, firefighters noticed that whenever they attended a fire, they would be

followed by men who were eager to watch them. Because these men wore buffalo fur to protect them against the cold, the firefighters started calling them buffalos, or buffs for short.

Why do women live longer than men?

It's undoubtedly true that women do live longer than men. They are, of course, physically and medically stronger: there is a lower incidence of infant mortality in girls than there is in boys, and women have a higher threshold of pain to withstand childbirth. However, is that enough to explain a four-year discrepancy in life expectancy?

According to the social anthropologist I consulted, it's mostly to do with lifestyle. 'If you look at the lives British men and women have led in the past 50 years, it's no wonder that men, who worked hard, commuted and suffered the consequent stress, died before their wives, who stayed at home, having smaller families and enjoying an increasing number of labour-saving devices. However, with the pattern of women's lives changing and becoming increasingly similar to men's in terms of work and recreation and consumption of tobacco and alcohol, there's every reason to believe that men's and women's life expectancy will become the same.' The facts bear this out: between 1970 and 2004, life expectancy at age 65 in England and Wales increased by four and a half years for men but only three and a half years for women.

Why is a non-drinker called a teetotaller?

There are two possibilities for this: the first is that when the word was first used – in Britain in the 1830s – it was describing 'total' abstinence and the 'tee' (echoing the first letter of 'total') was added for emphasis.

The other possibility – and the one that I much prefer – comes from a meeting of the Preston Temperance Society in 1832, in which a society member named Dickie Turner gave a speech in which he called for 'total abstinence'. However, because he had a stammer, he ended up calling for 't-t-t-total abstinence' and – or so the story goes – a word was born.

Why do we pour oil on troubled waters?

I confess that I have often been confused by the proverb 'To pour oil on troubled waters': does it mean to make things worse or to make them better. Having researched it, I discover that it means the latter. But that still begs the question: how? It turns out that oil would reduce the friction between the wind and the troubled waters and thus calm them.

OIL

Why do farts smell like rotten eggs?

Now let's get one thing absolutely straight: call it what you will – farting, blowing off, guffing, even the polite expression 'breaking wind' – everyone farts.

And I do mean *everyone* – even head teachers, Hollywood superstars and the Queen. All right, maybe not Her Majesty, but every other human and, I'm assuming, every mammal on the planet lets off from time to time.

And although, as Billy Connolly so famously pointed out, we all love the smell of our *own* farts – everyone else's smell horrible and usually of rotten eggs.

But why rotten eggs?

Well, it's because the protein in the food we eat is broken down into several chemicals – including hydrogen sulphide, which smells just like rotten eggs.

This compound is also found in well water and – yes, you've guessed it – rotten eggs!

Which is why . . .

Interestingly, the recognition threshold – the concentration at which 50% of humans can detect the characteristic smell of hydrogen sulphide – is 0.0047 ppm (parts per million).

Doesn't sound much but you wouldn't want any more in your system – no matter how much you liked your own farts: in greater concentration, hydrogen sulphide is a poison!

Why are people put through 'the third degree'?

. . . rather than the first or second? This refers to 'the third degree' that anyone undergoing thorough and relentless questioning experiences. It turns out that it's derived from the name given to the questioning that masons have to go through to progress in freemasonry.

What is Little Red Riding Hood's real name?

It had never occurred to me that she even had a real name until a reader wrote in to ask (saying that she thought it might be Brenda). So I did a little research and discovered that she did have a name but it wasn't Brenda – Maisie. According to the fairytale, her neighbours called her Little Red Riding Hood because of the scarlet riding hood and cloak (made for her by her grandmother) which she always wore.

Is it true that Good Friday once fell on Boxing Day?

Yes! But it's a trick question that refers to a horse named Good Friday which fell in a race held on 26 December 1899. So that's how Good Friday fell on Boxing Day!

If you were to fall out of an aeroplane high in the sky, would you be dead before you'd even hit the ground?

Almost certainly, according to my pet physicist. 'You'd speed up like Newton's apple,' he told me with relish, 'until you reached terminal velocity after about three hundred metres. The chances are that you'd die of heart failure – actually, to be precise, respiratory arrest – from the shock of your fall, so, yes, the chances are you'd be dead.'

However, there is hope in such circumstances, as I discovered when my research led me to Julianne Koepcke, who in 1971 fell two miles from an aeroplane after it lost control and lived to walk away.

How does a headache pill know to go to your head and not some other part of your body?

It doesn't! That's because it doesn't actually go to your head (or your foot or wherever you've got a pain). Instead, what it does – depending on the pill – is block pain or reduce inflammation.

The fact that it works on the headache doesn't mean that's where it goes though!

When did they stop executing people in the Tower of London?

I was amazed to discover that the answer is: as recently as 1941! Specifically, Thursday 14 August 1941, when Josef Jakobs, a German spy, was shot by an eight-man firing squad. Because Jakobs had broken his ankle when parachuting into England some seven months earlier, he was unable to stand before the firing squad and so he was seated in a chair instead and tied up before being shot five times in the heart.

Who was the first person to go on a properly planned slimming diet?

It was a London undertaker named William Banting in 1862. His scientifically planned slimming diet was devised by Dr Harvey, an ear specialist. Interestingly, at first dieting was something that men tended to do – women didn't start until they stopped wearing figure-altering corsets.

Why do we call someone a 'smart Alec' – as opposed to a smart Anthony or a smart Wayne?

Alex Hoag was a thief in the 1840s. He worked with his wife, Miranda, who would lure men into her room. Alex would slip into the room and steal the men's possessions. Alex would then return, posing as an angry jealous husband. The man would rush off, not caring that he'd been robbed. A smart Alex – or, as it became, Alec, or Aleck – indeed.

Why is a 'disc jockey' so called?

The term 'disc jockey' was coined in *Variety* back in 1937, describing radio announcers who stayed up all night 'riding' records.

Nowadays, disc jockeys are almost always called DJs.

Why do people touch wood for good luck?

Like so many superstitions and celebrations, this one has its roots in pagan times, when people worshipped trees – especially oak trees – and touched them for luck (or knocked them to drive out any evil spirits).

Later, after the life and death of Jesus Christ, people would touch wood for luck because Jesus' cross was made of wood.

Nowadays, many of us – atheists and agnostics included – touch wood routinely when we're hoping for something to happen or not happen.

Does SOS stand for Save Our Ship or Save Our Souls?

The answer is neither! SOS was chosen by an 1908 international conference on Morse Code simply because the letters S (dot dot dot) and O (dash dash dash) were so easy to remember. Afterwards, people tried to turn the letters into an acronym.

Why would Cinderella wear a glass slipper – wouldn't it have been uncomfortable?

Of course it would – but then it was a fairy story! However, in the original story, her slippers were fur: they became glass because of an error in translation.

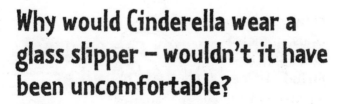

Why is it considered bad luck to kill a ladybird?

Apart from the fact that they are beautiful creatures and therefore deserve to be protected, they pose no direct danger to humans whatsoever. After all, when was the last time YOU were stung by a ladybird. However, the reason why it's considered unlucky to kill one is because the ladybird is said to represent the Virgin Mary, and you wouldn't want to mess with Jesus' mum!

Given that money can do great good, why is it described as 'the root of all evil'?

Of course money isn't, *per se*, the root of all evil, in fact, that so-called quotation is wrong. The Bible doesn't say that 'money is the root of all evil', it says 'For the love of money is the root of all evil.' In other words, money itself is fine – but don't worship it!

Why do ostriches stick their heads in the sand?

People who don't want to face up to some unpleasant fact are often accused of sticking their heads in the sand like an ostrich. In fact, the (simple) reason why ostriches stick their heads in the sand is because they're looking for water – not trying to avoid something.

WORK

Why is a wage-earner said to 'bring home the bacon'? Why not lamb or chicken?

In 16th-century Europe, being able to afford pork – or pig meat – was considered a sign of great wealth. So a man who could 'bring home the bacon' was more than providing for his family. When he entertained friends, he would cut off a piece of bacon or pork and give it to them to eat. They would sit around and (and this is where this saying is derived from) 'chew the fat'.

Why do people kiss under the mistletoe?

There are two sources for this practice. Firstly, as with so many Christmas traditions, it has its roots in pagan rituals – specifically, the kissing bough, which had mistletoe at its centre. When the Christmas tree replaced the kissing bough, the mistletoe was salvaged and introduced into the Yuletide ritual. Secondly, there is also the Norse legend of Baldur, who escaped being poisoned by mistletoe because his mother, Frigg, the goddess of love, removed the poison with her tears. Frigg was so happy that she kissed everyone who passed under the mistletoe – thus starting the custom.

In other words, any excuse for a kiss!

Is there a word which is plural but can be made singular by the adding of an S?

This is a real brainteaser! So don't look at the answer until you've thought about it for a while.

Given up?

OK then, here it is: the word 'princes' (plural) can become singular when you add an S to make 'princess'.

Why is money called 'bread'?

It's simple – it comes from Cockney rhyming slang: 'Give me your money. Give me your bread and honey.'

Were the 'three blind mice' in the nursery rhyme of the same name based on anything or anyone?

Yes. The three blind mice were the Protestant clergymen Thomas Cranmer, Hugh Latimer and Nicholas Ridley, whose death warrants were signed by Mary, Queen of Scots. The rhyme tells the story of their fate in the grisliest terms.

Why do we describe something that's ceased working properly as having 'gone to pot'?

Urns were once known as pots. If someone asked where a deceased person was, they were told that the individual had 'gone to pot' – in other words that they were in an urn. From there, the saying developed to include anyone or anything that's stopped working or is dead.

Why are hit films called 'blockbusters'?

A blockbuster was a bomb used in the Second World War in air raids on Germany which could destroy several buildings in a single explosion. From there, it was adopted by Hollywood publicists anxious to hype their films.

Is it known who – if anyone – wrote the piano piece Chopsticks?

Yes. It was actually registered at the British Museum 130 years ago – under the title *The Celebrated Chop Waltz*. Interestingly, the composer was listed as one 'Arthur de Lulli' but this turned out to be the pseudonym of a 16-year-old girl named Euphemia Allen. It is thought that this is the only piece of music she ever wrote.

What's the origin of the expression 'pig in a poke'?

If you buy a 'pig in a poke', the chances are you've been duped – been given something that's not worth the money you paid. It stems from the days when people selling pigs (or, more likely, piglets) in the market would take them along in a bag or 'poke'. These sellers would often be keen not to open their bags – ostensibly in case the animal escaped but also because it was possible that they were trying to pass off an inferior animal to an unwary purchaser who might 'let the cat out of the bag' (hence *that* expression). If someone bought a pig in a poke – i.e. unseen – he might very well come to regret it. The expression has come to represent an important legal saying: *caveat emptor,* or let the buyer beware. Especially when it comes to piglets concealed in bags . . .

Why are severe laws known as 'draconian'?

It's all because of a seventh-century BC Athenian lawmaker who decided that 'crimes' like laziness, vagrancy and petty theft should be punished by death. When asked why, Draco said, 'The smallest of them deserve death, and there is no greater punishment I can find for the greater crimes.' Draco himself died when, in an act of acclamation, his acolytes threw their hats and cloaks on top of him in a theatre – thereby suffocating him.

Were the nursery rhyme characters Jack and Jill actually based on anyone?

Yes. Jack represented the French king, Louis XVI, who 'lost his crown' in the Revolution, while Jill, who came 'tumbling after', was Marie Antoinette.

Why is a rabbit's foot lucky?

To which my immediate response is: 'Well, it wasn't lucky for the rabbit, was it?' In fact, it turns out that as long ago as the seventh century BC, rabbits were believed to have immunity when it came to evil forces and were also symbols of fertility. The latter is obviously fair enough but the former is simply wishful thinking.

Has anyone in living memory been sent to jail for blasphemy in Britain?

Well, I suppose it depends how long your memory is! In 1922 John Gott was sentenced to nine months' hard labour for comparing Christ's entry into Jerusalem to 'a circus clown on the back of two donkeys'. No one's been jailed for blasphemy since.

Why do Oriental people have different eyes to Europeans?

Oriental people don't have 'different eyes' to us Europeans or, more properly, us occidentals. Instead, they have an extra flap of skin – known as the epicanthic fold – that gives them a sort of double upper eyelid. Anthropologists aren't entirely sure but they reckon that it's to protect them against cold and glare. The thinking is that their forebears were trapped in Siberia by the glaciers during the last ice age; during that time, these people developed a number of physical traits that helped them cope with the bitter weather. Their noses became flattened to minimize exposure to the elements and reduce the risk of frostbite; their faces became round and flat and lined with fat, which acts as an insulator; on the same basis, their eyelids picked up a layer of fat as well.

WELCOME
TO
SIBERIA
ENJOY YOUR STAY

We've all heard the expression 'You could hear a pin drop', but could you?

According to my tame scientist, 'The sound energy in a pin drop is one quadrillionth of a watt, and moves the eardrum less than the diameter of a hydrogen molecule.' So could you actually *hear* it drop? 'Depends how good your hearing is, I suppose, but it's safe to say that no human being would be able to.' What about a dog? 'No – and before you proceed to run through the whole animal kingdom, I should say that no one and nothing could hear a pin drop. I think you'll find that that's the point of the expression.'

Is eating fish good for the brain?

We're often told that it is, and no less a man than P. G. Wodehouse's Jeeves attributed his brainpower to the eating of fish. But is it true? Well, according to scientists, yes, it is – but only up to a point. The brain needs decosahexaenoic acid to develop and this is found in oily fish, but beyond that fish has no extra 'brainy' properties not found in other sources of protein.

What's the cause of that bubbling you sometimes see at the top of ponds?

It's methane gas – produced by the decomposition of dead plants and animals in the mud.

What's the story behind the nursery rhyme 'Baa Baa Black Sheep'?

It has its roots in the Middle Ages, when ordinary people found themselves having to hand over money not only to the king but also to the local aristocrat. So the song – almost certainly the first protest song about tax – complains about having to give one 'full bag' to the master (the king), one to the dame (the aristocracy), with only the last bag going to the producer himself, characterized as 'the little boy who lives down the lane'.

WOOL
WOOL

What are the origins of Rudolph, the red-nosed reindeer?

Rudolph was created as recently as 1939 for a Christmas promotion for the Montgomery Ward department store in Chicago. The words were written as a poem by Robert May, an advertising copywriter, but music wasn't added until 1947 – by which time May had persuaded the store to let him have the rights to the character. In 1949 Gene Autry recorded the song and had a massive hit with it.

Do Scotsmen wear anything under their kilts?

According to a Scottish friend I asked – a regular kilt-wearer: 'No, not if they're real Scotsmen.'

But what if the wind blows your kilt over your head . . . ?

'We wear special shirts that have long tails. On an especially windy day, we might tie up those tails to protect our modesty. But don't tell anyone that, OK?'

Your secret is safe with me . . . and my readers!

Which was the first city to be 'twinned' with a city abroad?

It was Coventry, which was twinned with Stalingrad (now Volgograd) during the Second World War.

This was, as far as I can tell, not just the first twinning for a British city but for *any* two cities anywhere in the world.

It came about when women from Coventry embroidered their names on a huge table-cloth and sent it to the women of Stalingrad – a city that was under siege by the Germans.

From that start, the two cities became twinned.

After the war, Coventry, a city which was devastated by German bombs, was twinned with Dresden, which had likewise been destroyed by the Allies, in an act of reconciliation.

You're an old man, Mitch, so what's your best advice?

- Learn from the mistakes of others: you won't live long enough to make them all yourself.

- Never underestimate the power of stupid people in large groups.

- Don't condemn other people's opinions: you might both be wrong.

- Talk slowly but think quickly.

- Don't worry about making mistakes: they're the price you pay for living a full life.

- Forget injuries but never forget kindnesses.

- When you're asked how you are, say 'I'm well,' NOT 'I'm good.'

Never walk up the down escalator.

Never laugh at your own jokes.

Never shop in a store that won't let you use its toilet.

Don't take chocolates from the lower layer until you've finished all the chocolates on the top layer.

Never eat yellow snow.

Take care not to bore people.

- If in doubt, tell the truth.

- Respect the personal space of large growling animals.

- Don't be embarrassed by bodily functions.

- Don't feel obliged to read a book all the way through just because you've started it (even this one).

- Never say 'In my humble opinion'.

- Never wear a baseball cap back to front unless you want to shrink your IQ.

- Take chances: if you don't risk anything, you risk even more.

- The two hardest things to handle in life are failure and success.

- Never miss a good chance to shut up.

Apologize when you're in the wrong – and look the person you're apologizing to in the eye.

Never visit a funfair on a full stomach.

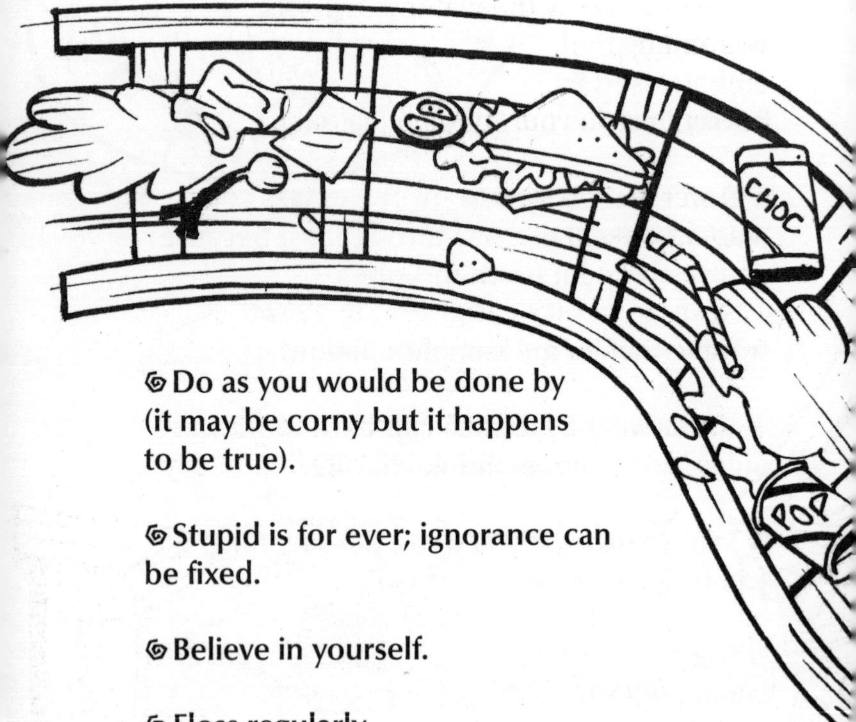

Do as you would be done by (it may be corny but it happens to be true).

Stupid is for ever; ignorance can be fixed.

Believe in yourself.

Floss regularly.

- Allow others to discover your good qualities without your help.

- Generally speaking, you aren't learning much when your mouth is moving.

- Never swallow the water in a public swimming pool.

- Don't waste your time on jealousy.

- Never look down on anyone unless you're helping them up.

- Never forget it's easier to stay out of trouble than to get out of trouble.

- Don't bother saving for a rainy day as the chances are you'll stay in that day.

Never try to teach a pig to sing. It wastes your time and annoys the pig.

Never play leapfrog with a unicorn.

Never answer someone else's mobile phone.

Never have a staring match with an owl.

Never tie your shoelaces in a revolving door.

Never argue with an idiot. Bystanders can't tell the difference.

Never, ever make absolute, unconditional statements.

If you and your friend are being chased by a mad dog, don't worry about out-running the mad dog, just worry about out-running your friend.

Never wipe your bottom with a hedgehog.

Eat a live mouse in the morning and nothing worse will happen to you for the rest of the day.

We can't all be heroes because somebody has to stand and clap as they go by.

People who say 'It's the luck of the draw' usually did better in the draw than you.

Good judgement comes from experience. Experience comes as a result of bad judgement.

Why were the Egyptian mummies so called?

It had nothing to do with mothers! They were called mummies because of the wax – or 'mum' – that was smeared on to the bandages for waterproofing purposes.

What's the origin of the expression 'To get someone's goat'?

If you 'get someone's goat', you upset them. This comes from the practice of keeping a goat in a stable with a racehorse as a companion. If someone wanted to nobble the horse before a race, then they might steal their goat companion. In other words, they'd 'got their goat' and therefore upset the horse (and, presumably, its owner!).

Has any company inadvertently adopted an unfortunate website address?

Alas for them (but happily for us), lots of companies have unwittingly found themselves with daft website addresses. Some of the results are too rude for a book like this but do please consider the mess that the following – perfectly innocent – got themselves into . . .

www.choosespain.com

www.ipanywhere.com

www.speedofart.com

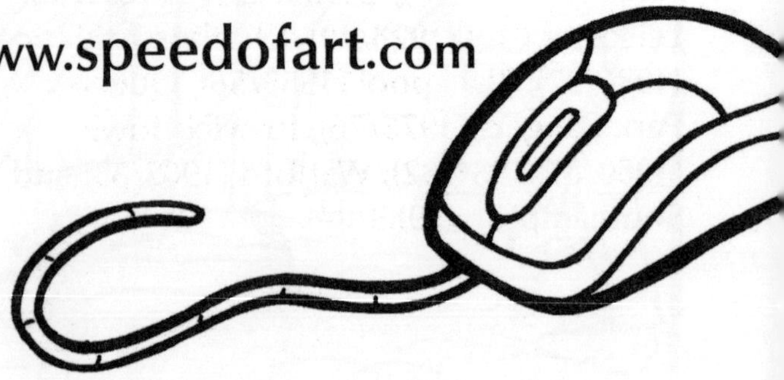

Has any football club finished runner-up in the Premiership (or old First Division) without ever winning the title?

I wouldn't have thought that would have happened to any club, but then maybe I'm just so used to Arsenal, Liverpool, Manchester United and Chelsea carving up the top spots among themselves.

Consequently, I was surprised to find that the following clubs all finished second in the top flight without ever subsequently going on to win the title: Bristol City (1906/7), Oldham Athletic (1914/15), Cardiff City (1923/24), Leicester City (1928/29), Charlton Athletic (1936/37), Blackpool (1955/56), Queen's Park Rangers (1975/76), Ipswich Town (1980/81; 1981/82), Watford (1982/83) and Southampton (1983/84).

Is it cheaper to keep a horse than it is to run a car?

Depends on the type of car and where someone lives and what kind of journeys they do!

A cheap car costs a minimum of £2,000 a year to keep on the road while a more expensive car will cost double that to run.

Horses cost much less than most cars – £3,000 will buy a perfectly good, sensible horse. But oh dear, the running costs are *much* higher. Unless you have a field next to your house which you can use for free (which of course most people don't), a field and stable and someone to look after it will cost about the same as running a Renault for a year. Plus, you must add in a horse's shoes, which cost about £10 a week (more if they wear them out on the hard roads – which,

if they were replacing a car, they surely would). Then there are vets' bills, and of course there are times when the horse wouldn't be well enough to work or when the weather was too grim to ride in.

So all in all, horses these days are still more expensive to run than cars.

Consider, if you will, one more piece of evidence: if the price of petrol goes up, so does the cost of transporting food. And that's without factoring in problems like the price of grain going up or, after a very wet summer, the cost of hay and straw increasing.

There are advantages, however, for people who swap their cars for horses. Horses are gorgeous animals and will lick your hand in a way that no motor car ever would or could.

They're good for the environment and, best of all, no horse ever set off a speed camera!

However, you might well have a nasty accident. Horses are powerful animals; they are easily frightened and can panic, especially close to fast-moving traffic or if they hear sudden loud noises. Accurate statistics for road accidents involving horses are not available, but the British Horse Society thinks that there are at least 3,000 such accidents every year – about half of which occur on minor roads like country lanes. This is why drivers are asked to 'Slow Down For Horses'. If only more would!

Does Britain still have any (populated) dependent territories?

There was a time when Britannia ruled the waves, a quarter of the world was controlled by Britain and the sun never set on the British Empire, but nowadays there are very few countries that have 'dependent territory' status.

In fact, the only ones that do are: Bermuda (population of 64,000), the Cayman Islands (46,000), Gibraltar (28,000), the Turks & Caicos Islands (21,000), the British Virgin Islands (21,000), Anguilla (12,000), Montserrat (9,000), St Helena (6,000), the Falkland Islands (3,000) and Pitcairn Island (50 – that's right, just 50, according to the latest figures I could find, which were from 2007).

Can anyone buy a black cab – like the sort that London taxi drivers use?

I checked on this and it turns out that anyone – any adult, that is! – can buy a London taxi, but obviously they can't 'ply for hire' until and unless they become licensed taxi drivers. Stephen Fry, Prince Philip, Lord Andrew Lloyd Webber, Michael Jackson, Kate Moss and Keith Allen have all bought black cabs for their own personal use – presumably because they don't want people to notice them, but also perhaps because black cabs are renowned for their reliability and incredibly tight turning circle.

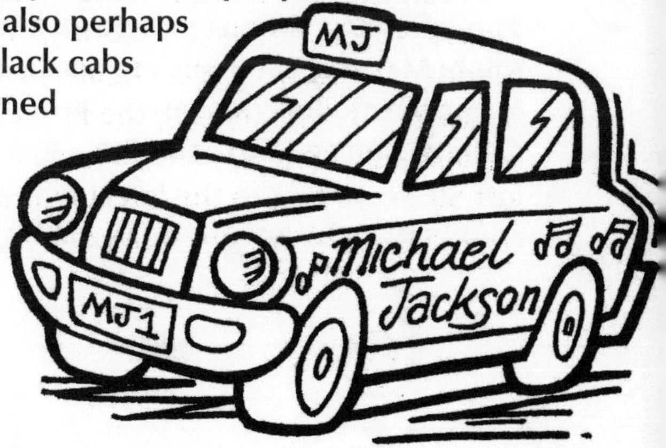

What does it mean if a person has 'perfect pitch'?

It means that they have the ability to sing or recognize the pitch of a tone or a song by ear. The easiest way to find out if you have perfect pitch is to listen to some notes on a piano then go away for a few minutes. If, when you return, you can identify the notes – played at random – then you might very well have it. Similarly, you could try singing a (recorded) song you know well and then play that song and see if you're in tune with it.

The following famous people all have perfect pitch: Mariah Carey, Michael Jackson, Bill Bailey, Dame Julie Andrews, Barbra Streisand, Celine Dion and Tina Turner.

Has any former slave gone on to become famous?

Quite a few! Miguel de Cervantes, the author of *Don Quixote*, was a slave in the Barbary States. St Patrick, the patron saint of Ireland, was abducted from Britain and enslaved in Ireland. He later escaped but then returned to Ireland as a missionary. Aesop, the author, famous for his fables, was a slave on the island of Samos; but perhaps the most famous slave of all time was Spartacus, who led a slaves' revolt against the Roman Empire.

Is there any benefit – besides the taste – to eating chocolate?

Do you want the good news or the bad news?

All right, the good news is that there are plenty of benefits to eating chocolate. The bad news, however, is that this only applies to chocolate that's high in cocoa content (60%+) and that almost certainly means plain chocolate, which is less sweet and more bitter than milk chocolate. I love plain chocolate but it's what they call an acquired taste and I hated it as a child.

Anyway, here are the benefits of eating chocolate:

- Chocolate can help reduce persistent coughing.

- Chocolate has been used for hundreds of years to treat diarrhoea.

- Chocolate releases serotonin in the brain which produces feelings of pleasure.

- Chocolate stimulates pleasure-giving endorphins which can help with pain relief.

- Chocolate increases brain activity.

- However, unless you want to end up as fat as me, don't eat too much of it!

Why might someone be described as being 'as mad as a hatter'?

You've probably heard of the Mad Hatter who appears in *Alice in Wonderland*. However, Lewis Carroll, the book's author, didn't invent the idea of the hatter as a mad person.

For this we have to look at the work that the hatter did.

He made hats for a living – many of which were made out of felt. Unfortunately for him, the mercury – or, more specifically, the mercury compound – that he used in the process was a poison that had the effect of literally driving him mad.

Hence the expression.

Why do we 'chance our arm' when we take a risk? Why not our leg or some other part of our body?

There are two perfectly good explanations for this – and I'll give them both to you so you can make up your own mind which one you prefer.

The first is that it comes from boxing. When a boxer extends his fist to hit his opponent, he is leaving himself vulnerable to counter-attack. In that way, he's chancing his arm.

The other possibility is that it refers to a soldier – specifically a corporal or a sergeant – doing something that might get him into trouble and lead to him being demoted and therefore having his stripes removed from the arm of his tunic. In that way he would be chancing his arm.

I have to say that I prefer the first explanation – probably because it's more literal – but the second comes from an earlier time (the 19th century rather than the 20th century) and so might be the true origin of the expression.

Who first thought of popping corn to make popcorn?

Popcorn dates back at least 5,000 years. Ears of corn found in caves in America's New Mexico dated from that period. In Peruvian tombs 1,000 years old, popcorn kernels have been found in such a good state of preservation that they'd still pop.

Popcorn is thought to have originated in Mexico but was also grown in China,

Sumatra and India before the Americas were even discovered. Native Americans offered popcorn to the European settlers as a peace-offering. In the 1700s, colonial housewives began to serve popcorn with cream and sugar as an early form of 'sugar puff' cereal. Most of the world's poppable corn is still grown in America – where they prefer it salted: in Britain and Europe, we prefer it sweetened.

Each kernel of corn contains a small drop of water stored inside a circle of soft starch. When the corn is heated, the water expands and pressurizes the starch into collapsing, causing the popcorn to explode. The explosion turns the kernel inside out, releasing steam and the popcorn is popped. Nowadays, kernels that don't pop are called 'old maids' and are usually thrown away as 'duds'. However, experts at the American Popcorn Board in Chicago say these can be rejuvenated simply by re-hydrating the dried kernels.

Popcorn was first sold on the streets of America in the 1890s, when street vendors would go from parks and street corners to funfairs and exhibitions to sell popped corn.

During the Great Depression in the 1930s, popcorn was one of the few luxuries that even the poor could afford. So while other businesses failed, popcorn thrived. One Oklahoma banker whose bank went bust bought a mobile popcorn machine and started a small business in a store near a theatre. The story goes that three years later his popcorn business had made him enough money to buy back three of the farms he had lost in the Depression.

Butterkist, the best-known brand, was launched in Britain in 1938 and its factory in Dagenham, Essex, went on to become the largest and most advanced of its kind in the world.

Popcorn can be served in many ways – salted, sweetened with caramel or sugar, plain or even with cheese or fruit. Butterkist is made with maple and pecan, toffee or banoffi flavours as well as plain or salted. Although popcorn seems fattening, even the buttered or nutty varieties are lower in calories than their equivalent weight in crisps or chocolate.

Why do boys' voices 'break' when they get into their teens?

When a boy is about 13 or 14, his vocal cords start lengthening. When they finish, he'll have a deep voice like his father and other men. However, for a couple of years during this process, his voice may be all over the place. This might sound funny but it can be very embarrassing for the boys concerned.

Girls' vocal cords, on the other hand, don't alter very much – if at all – and that's why adults often mistake a young boy for a girl on the telephone!

Why is Latin America so called?

Latin America is basically all the countries in Central and South America where Spanish or Portuguese is spoken. These are, of course, both languages that are based on Latin.

Interestingly though, the term Latin America is not that old – it goes back only to the middle of the 19th century, when the French Emperor Napoleon III was attempting to bring the region under French control. As far as he was concerned, since the Latin languages obviously included French, this would possibly help him to persuade influential people in the area to think of Latin America as a region where the French had a legitimate interest.

What's that smell you smell when you go to the seaside?

That smell is possibly my favourite smell (apart from maybe a particularly pungent rose) and the main reason why I chose to live right next to the sea.

I always thought it was ozone but recently I read that it's a gas named dimethyl sulphide which is produced by microbes in the ocean.

The trouble is that this gas isn't the fill-your-lungs-with-that-it's-good-for-you stuff that ozone is; once again, I've discovered that something I love is, in fact, not particularly good for me.

Bah!

Why is a lowly person called a dogsbody?

I don't know if you've ever seen any episodes of the brilliant TV comedy *Blackadder*, but there's a character in that named Baldrick and he is – was – the absolute epitome of a dogsbody.

Put upon by his master – Blackadder – in all his incarnations, no job was too low or disgusting for this poor man. He was, if you like, the dogsbody's dogsbody.

This wonderfully evocative word has its roots in the Royal Navy of the 19th century. One of the ghastly foods that British sailors were given to eat was pease pudding (a sort of dried peas concoction). The sailors, however, called it dog's body – possibly because of the shape of the bag the peas came in. Over time, the sort of sailor who had to eat this food and the food's nickname became one.

Eventually, the word dogsbody was used to describe any underling who always got the grottiest jobs.

A real example – if ever there was one – of 'you are what you eat'!

Why is wee-wee sometimes yellow and sometimes clear?

Wee-wee – or urine, to give it its proper name – is the way in which the body (or, to be more specific, the kidneys) flushes out impurities. It should be fairly clear in colour but if you haven't drunk enough water recently, then it might turn yellow – simply because the waste you're getting rid of isn't as diluted as it should be.

Think of it like orange squash and you'll see what I mean.

But don't – whatever you do – *treat* it like orange squash . . .

How do they get wooden ships into glass bottles?

Remarkably simply – although it is a delicate operation. First of all they make the model ship but they ensure that the sails and mast are collapsible. They insert the whole ship into the bottle and then, once it's inside, they pull on a piece of string that is attached to the sails and mast and raise the rigging. After this, all they have to do is unloop the piece of string and, bingo, they've got a ship that's bigger than the neck of the bottle into the bottle!

What's so special about the number 23?

There's always been a lot of mystique about the number 23. It's not just considered a lucky number (there are plenty of those in many different societies and cultures), it's also deeply significant to many people.

But why:

- Well, there are lots of reasons and I'll list as many as I can but, of all of them, I think it's because of the beauty of the 23rd Psalm, the one that starts with the line 'The Lord is my shepherd'.

Here are other possible reasons for the number's significance:

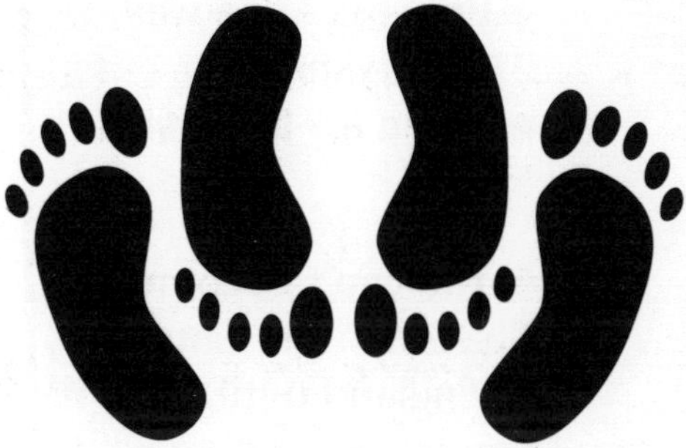

- Parents each contribute 23 chromosomes to start a new human life during reproduction

- There are 23 letters in the Latin alphabet.

- 23 is the first prime number in which both digits are also primes and add up to another prime.

. . . and here are some more examples of the number's significance:

- Julius Caesar was stabbed 23 times.

23 is the lowest number you can achieve with just one dart.

Princess Anne was 23 when she got married for the first time.

You can't become a deacon in the Church of England until you're 23.

The New York subway system has 23 different lines.

The eighth rib – the eighth longest bone in the human body – measures 23 cm.

The human biorhythm is generally 23 days.

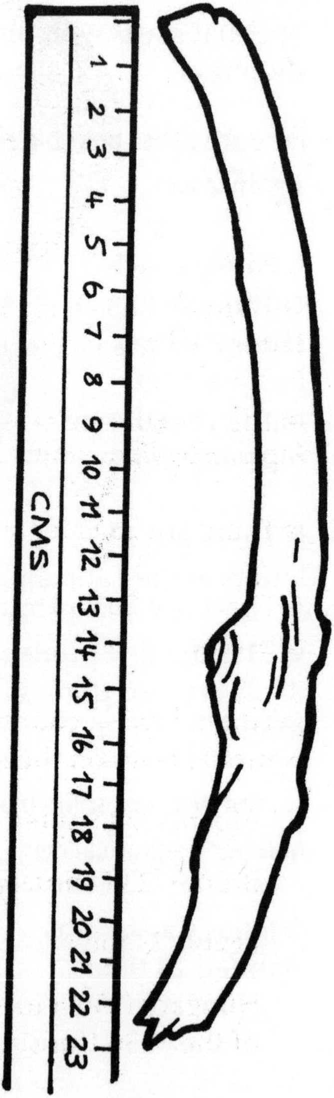

There are 23 characters (numbers and letters) on the faces of US coins.

The Nissan car takes its name from the Japanese *NI*, meaning 2, and *SAN*, meaning 3.

There are 23 categories of Academy Awards.

There are 23 towns in the US called Moscow.

The following countries celebrate their National Days on the 23rd of a month:

Albania (23 September)

Brunei (23 February)

Egypt (23 July)

Hungary (23 October – the anniversary of the 1956 Uprising)

Japan (23 December – the emperor's birthday)

Luxembourg (23 June)

Pakistan (23 March)

Saudi Arabia (23 September)

- Dr Pepper is advertised as having 23 flavours.

- The European Union has 23 official languages.

- The human brain contains roughly 23 billion neurons, each linked to as many as 10,000 other neurons.

- Michael Jordan wore the number 23 – so does David Beckham for LA Galaxy.

- 23 is the fifth of the mystical numbers in the TV series *Lost*.

- *Sesame Street*'s Bert is a member of the National Association of W Lovers, the 23rd letter of the alphabet.

It takes 23 seconds for blood to circulate through the human body.

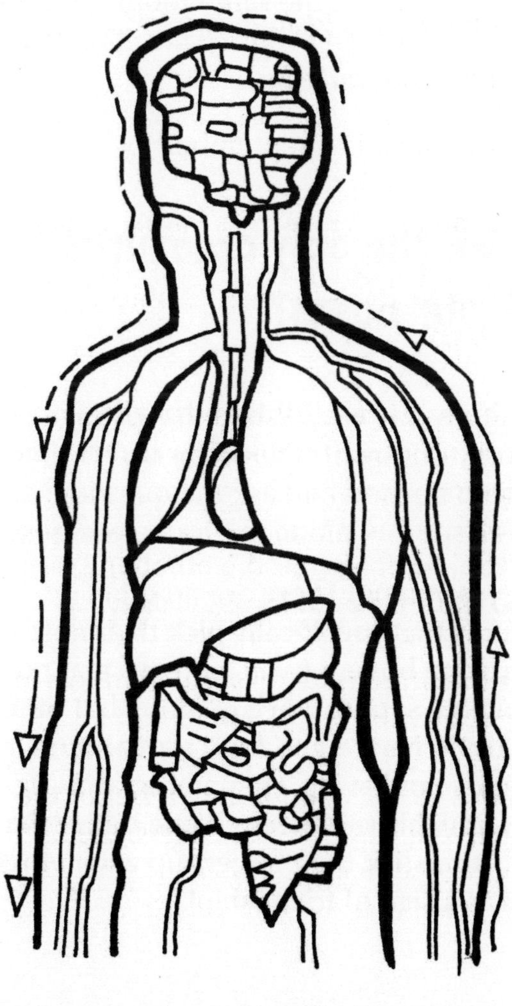

As readers of *Why Eating Bogeys Is Good For You* will know, you only have to have 23 or more people in the same room for there to be a better than evens chance that two share the same birthday.

Are we the only creatures to pick our noses?

Having already established that eating bogeys (but only our own) is good for us, it's time to go a step beyond and ask the question: are we, as a species, alone in picking our noses?

Well, yes and no. There are no other creatures that specifically pick their noses to excavate bogeys (which proves that nose-picking is a superior occupation), but other animals do have a good old root around in the course of having a general scratch. In fact, Capuchin monkeys go one better than we do and stick their fingers up each other's noses as a sign of friendship!

Is there anyone famous whose name is entirely made up of letters each worth just one point in Scrabble?

As regular Scrabble players will know, the following letters are each worth one point:

A E I L N O R S T and U.

My own name has many letters that are worth more than one – M(3), C(3), H(4), Y(4) and M again. I'm sure yours does too.

So it's a tough challenge to find famous names that only contain letters worth one point each.

I found the following:

TS Eliot (poet)

Stan Laurel (of Laurel and Hardy fame)

Laurie Lee (author)

Tea Leoni (actress)

Lulu (singer)

Ilie Nastase (tennis player)

Nero (Roman emperor)

Leslie Nielsen (actor)

Aristotle Onassis (shipping tycoon)

Luise Rainer (double-Oscar winning actress)

Roseanne (actress and comedienne)

Rene Russo (actress)

Alan Sillitoe (author)

Neil Tennant (pop star)

Stella Tennant (model)

Tina Turner (singer)

Do you know anyone who falls into this category? It's great fun working it out, I can tell you!

Who invented fireworks?

That's impossible to say – but it would have been someone in China!

Fireworks were invented by accident by the Chinese over a thousand years ago. One theory is that the explosives were discovered as monks attempted to find the Elixir of Life – the secret to longevity or long life.

The other is that cooks came across the recipe in their kitchens. The former seems the more probable explanation as it is hard to imagine something edible being made from the basic ingredients of sulphur, saltpetre (potassium nitrate) and charcoal.

The Chinese packed the mixture into sticks of bamboo, jammed the end with river mud and set fire to them, with spectacular results – showers of gold and silver accompanied by cracking sounds. They used their 'arrows of flying fire' in ceremonies and also to ward off evil sprits.

In Europe, several centuries later, fireworks became an everyday part of religious celebrations and processions in the Catholic countries of Spain, France and Italy. The Crusaders most probably brought them back from the East. Italian and French chemists experimented with different chemicals and came up with an array of colours by adding potassium chlorate to a range of metal salts. Barium made green, sodium made yellow, while strontium made red. They also introduced special effects. Blue eluded them for centuries until it was realized that copper would produce the colour.

By the 1500s, the spectacle appealed so much to Europe's kings and queens, it became commonplace for fireworks to be used to mark declarations of peace, victory, war and any big royal occasion. The French kings were particularly enthusiastic and used them for royal weddings as well as for theatrical events. Henry VIII and Elizabeth I commissioned displays for private and state occasions and appointed a Fireworks Master. George II was the first to add music when he commissioned Handel to compose a special outdoor concerto in the early 18th century.

In Britain, before 1872 it was illegal to make fireworks and the occupation was dangerous not only for liberty, but also for life. People would dry out explosive ingredients using an open fire and store volatile chemicals in their loft, with often disastrous consequences. One spark could blow up the whole of a tightly packed street. But politicians and royalty often turned a blind eye to the illegal trade, mainly because they wanted fireworks for their own events.

Once the manufacture of fireworks became legal, people were keen to use them at every opportunity. One day was particularly popular: 5 November – as it was the anniversary of the Gunpowder Plot, when Guy Fawkes and his accomplices tried to blow up Parliament.

Modern fireworks work by mixing gunpowder with various ingredients, such as magnesium, titanium, barium and aluminium. When they are lit, the chemical reactions create a mass of different colours and effects.

Why are primary colours called primary?

Red, blue, and yellow are called primary colours because just by mixing any two or three of them, you can create all the colours in the spectrum.

Is it really true that a butterfly flapping its wings in China can cause a hurricane in Britain?

Fortunately not! But then why even ask the question? Ah, that's slightly more complicated. The reason why people claim that the actions of a butterfly (or any tiny creature) can have such devastating effects is because they're trying to illustrate the

idea that small changes can produce large, unexpected results. It's called 'Chaos Theory' and it's a way of looking at how different things interact with each other and lead on to bigger events. It's the mathematical version of that extraordinary poem, *For Want of a Nail* which dates back to 14th-century England:

For want of a nail the shoe was lost.
For want of a shoe the horse was lost.
For want of a horse the rider was lost.
For want of a rider the battle was lost.
For want of a battle the kingdom was lost.
And all for the want of a horseshoe nail.

Was there really an old woman who lived in a shoe?

You know the old nursery rhyme:

There was an old woman who lived in a shoe.
She had so many children, she didn't know what to do.
She gave them some broth without any bread,
Then whipped them all soundly and put them to bed.

Obviously, no woman actually lived in a shoe with her (eight) children! It would, after all, have to be a VERY large shoe.

Instead, like so many nursery rhymes, it has its origins in mockery and goes back to the reign of King George II. That much we know, but there's some debate about whether the nursery rhyme is mocking him (he wore a white wig and was teased – behind his back – for looking like an old woman) and the politicians (children) who did whatever he told them to do, or is mocking his wife, Queen Caroline II, who bore him eight children.

Why is a boxing ring so called?

Point taken! After all, a boxing ring is square, or at least rectangular: so why call it a ring? The simple answer is that boxing rings used to be round. That's it.

By the way, while we're on the subject of boxing, here's a fantastic trick/logic question to ask family and friends:

If a boxing match takes place over 15 rounds, each taking three minutes, and there's a one-minute break between rounds, how long does the contest last (assuming it goes the full 15 rounds)?

Almost everyone you ask will multiply 15 (rounds) by 3 (minutes) and then add another 15 for the one-minute breaks – giving them a total of 60. But the correct answer is 59. Why? Well, there are only 14 one-minute breaks as they don't have one after the 15th round because the fight's over!

Why isn't cricket played at the Olympics?

Probably because not enough countries play it – well, not enough countries at a high enough standard.

The fact is that cricket is only played at Test level – i.e. the highest level – by countries that used to be part of the British Empire. So the only Test playing countries are England, Australia, South Africa, the West Indies, India, Pakistan, New Zealand, Sri Lanka, Zimbabwe and Bangladesh. It simply wouldn't be fair on all the other countries in the world!

That being said, there was once an Olympic cricket match. It took place in 1900 and a club team from England beat a team of British men who were based in France and were representing that country. England won so can therefore claim to be the current Olympic cricket champions!

Why are CAPITAL LETTERS and small letters sometimes called UPPER CASE and lower case?

They're terms used in printing. Before computers, all print had to be set in individual letters by hand. The printer kept all the letters in a case with the capital (or upper case) letters stored at the top (or upper end) of the case and the small (or lower) letters stored at the bottom (or lower end) of the case.

Does peanut butter actually contain any butter?

Despite its name, it doesn't! But it's called peanut butter because of the buttery taste of the peanuts when they're mashed to a pulp.

Peanut butter was developed by Dr John Harvey Kellogg (yes, *that* Kellogg) for his patients at the Battle Creek Sanatorium in Michigan at the end of the 19th century. He copied the recipe from another American physician, Dr Ambrose Straub, who had been prescribing ground-up peanuts as a paste for his elderly patients with bad teeth. He in turn had discovered that the Incas of South America had been eating a paste made from peanuts for centuries.

The paste was highly nutritious – being higher in protein than poultry, meat, fish or bread. Indeed, a typical jar of peanut butter has as much protein as 12 eggs or 12 glasses of milk. It was also full of energy so it was ideal for convalescents who needed building up.

Peanut butter didn't arrive in Britain until 1930. Sun-Pat was the first brand and is still the biggest. The process of making it was quite simple – the peanuts were shelled and then roasted before being ground into a smooth paste and mixed with sugar, salt and a stabilizer to prevent the peanut oil from separating and rising to the top of the jar. By law, peanut butter must contain at least 90% peanuts with no artificial additives, flavours, colours or sweeteners.

Peanuts may taste like nuts but they are actually from the bean family and grow underground rather than on trees. Most of the world's peanuts come from the Deep South of the United States, but they're also grown in South America, China, West Africa, India and Australia.

In Britain, about a quarter of the population eats peanut butter, and the crunchy variety is more popular than the smooth, although children usually prefer the smooth as it tends to stick less to their teeth. The reason it sticks is because the high level of protein draws the moisture from the mouth. Some people actually believe that peanut butter makes a good substitute for toothpaste.

In the US, where half the 1.6 million-ton annual peanut crop is used to make peanut butter, it is estimated that the average teenager has eaten more than 1,500 peanut butter sandwiches before leaving high school – usually mixed with jam (what they call 'jelly').

Why 'the life of Riley'?

Someone who's having an easy time is often described as 'leading (or having) the life of Riley'.

So who was this lucky chap?

The expression has its origins in the 1890 song 'Is That Mr Reilly?'. The song was about a Mr Reilly and what he would do if only he were wealthy (in the song Riley says that if he ever became the President of the US, then New York would 'swim in wine when the White House and Capitol are mine' and 'a hundred a day would be my pay'). Now fade to black and fade up again. In 1919 there was a music-hall song entitled 'My Name Is Kelly', which had the line 'Faith and my name is Kelly, Michael Kelly, but I'm living the life of Reilly just the same.' That's to say, the life of Reilly (or, as it became, Riley) as set down in the earlier song. Interestingly, the original song's chorus went, 'Are you the O'Reilly who keeps this hotel? Are you the O'Reilly they speak of so well? Are you the O'Reilly they speak of so highly, Gor Blime O'Reilly, you're looking well.' This is thought to be the origin of the expression 'Blimey O'Riley'.

Two phrases derived from one song: there's good value for you. In the interests of fair play (and to show off my scholarship), I should point out that there was an American poet by the name of James Whitcomb Riley who some people say is responsible for 'the life of Riley' as he wrote poems about young boys lazing around during the summer, swimming and fishing. I prefer the first explanation.

Who invented Play-Doh?

Play-Doh, the popular modelling clay, was invented in 1955 by brothers Joseph and Noah McVicker of Cincinnati, Ohio. Their company, Kutol Chemicals, produced a wallpaper cleaner called Cincy, but it wasn't selling well until, one day, Joseph's sister, a nursery school teacher, gave him an idea.

Her pupils didn't like the standard modelling clay because it was too heavy to manipulate and mould. So, instead, she let them use Cincy wallpaper cleaner and they found it worked brilliantly.

Unfortunately, Cincy had one big drawback: it stank. So the McVickers added almond perfume to the off-white goop, giving it its distinctive scent, and took their invention to an educational convention, where a department store bought some for their toy department.

It soon became a huge seller and a big success.

If all the Play-Doh made since 1955 were extruded through the Fun Factory, it would make a 'snake' that would wrap around the world nearly 300 times.

Why are we said to 'pay through the nose' when we're paying too much?

In the 17th century, 'rhino' was a popular slang word for money, while 'rhinos' is the Greek word for 'nose'. From there, the connection is easy to see.

Now consider the following limerick:

There was a young man of Montrose,
Who had pockets in none of his clothes.
When asked by his lass
Where he carried his brass,
He said, 'Darling, I pay through the nose.'

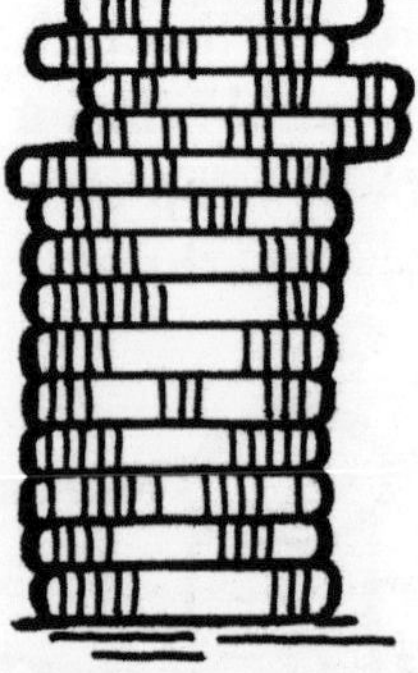

Is it true that we should each drink eight glasses of water a day?

No it's not! The idea that we should came from a nutritionist's report saying that each of us probably consumes the equivalent of eight glasses of water a day – from all the food and drink we get through in a day. From there, people went away with the misunderstanding that we had to drink eight glasses of water each day.

Having said that, it is important to drink plenty of water.

Is Scissors Paper Stone just a game of chance or is there a way to ensure victory?

On one level, Scissors Paper Stone is just a simple playground game in which scissors cut paper which wraps stone which blunts scissors.

So, yes, you can just select a symbol at random (known as 'Chaos' play) but there are also strategies to help you win.

The easiest is to select stone on the first turn. Why? Because the game is called Scissors Paper Stone and so almost everyone chooses scissors for the first turn. Your stone will blunt their scissors.

Before I move on to other strategies, I'd like to tell you more about this fascinating game, which has a long history.

It started in China before being exported to Japan where it was played with the utmost seriousness by the Samurai warriors in the

16th century. They would select a 'changer', who would set the challenge for the rest by standing in front of them saying, 'Jan, ken, pon,' three times. At the last 'jan, ken, pon,' the changer would make either scissors, paper or stone and the other Samurai would win or lose based on the choices they made.

The practice of saying 'Jan, ken, pon' before revealing the choice (rather like the 'Ick, ack, ock' sometimes used in Britain, the 'Ching chang chong' used in Germany or the 'Roe, sham, boe' occasionally used in North America) led to the game being called Janken in Japan.

In North America and Canada where the game is extremely popular, Stone is called Rock. In Japan, they also play Snake Frog Slug and Warrior Tiger Warrior's Mother and Fire Snake Water. In Indonesia, they play Elephant Human Ant. In Vietnam, they play Hammer Nail Wrapping. In France, they have four symbols instead of three: Rock, Leaf, Scissors and Well. Well beats rock and scissors, because both of them sink in the well. Scissors beats leaf, because it can cut leaves. Leaf beats well by covering it, and beats rock by wrapping it up. Rock beats scissors by blunting them.

There are Scissors Paper Stone tournaments held all over the world. From these some distinct strategies have emerged.

Chaos Play: Players select symbols randomly on the basis that an opponent can't know what you're going to do when you yourself don't know. Critics of this strategy insist that there's no such thing as a random throw: there's always *some* reason for choosing a symbol.

Gambit Play: Players select a series of three symbols in advance and then use them. This stops them from being influenced by their opponents. There are, of course, only 27 possible gambits but they can be used like building blocks so that if you're playing a lot, you can combine two or more. Here are the eight most widely used.

Avalanche (Stone Stone Stone)

Bureaucrat (Paper Paper Paper)

Crescendo (Paper Scissors Stone)

Dénouement (Stone Scissors Paper)

Fistful o' Dollars (Stone Paper Paper)

Paper Dolls (Paper Scissors Scissors)

Scissor Sandwich (Paper Scissors Paper)

Toolbox (Scissors Scissors Scissors)

Exclusion Play: Players discard one of the three symbols and never use it – the thinking being that your opponent will focus their entire strategy on predicting when the missing throw will appear – even if it never appears at all.

Whatever strategy you choose, make sure you *never* tell your opponent beforehand or else you'll never win!

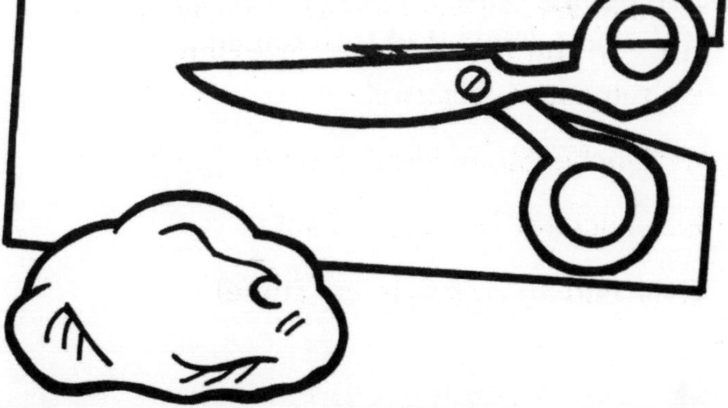

Why are Australian women sometimes referred to as 'Sheilas'?

According to an Aussie pal of mine, 'One theory dates back to when convicts were transported to Australia. Male prisoners were called "lags" and female prisoners were called "she-lags". A more likely explanation is that a large number of Irish people emigrated to Australia of their own free will, especially during the 19th-century potato famine. Sheila was a very popular Irish name and it may have just become a generic word for all women. Did you know, by the way, that Australia still has the largest population of Irish people outside of Ireland and that 35% of the population is of Irish origin?'

How come Israel is allowed to enter the Eurovision Song Contest?

Tough question; simple answer. According to the BBC, although Israel isn't a European country, it is a member of the European Broadcasting Union – the sole criterion for entry to the contest. Other member countries include Jordan, Libya and Morocco, but Arab countries traditionally tended not to enter because of Israel's involvement. Israel won in 1978 and 1979. Winning the contest confers the dubious (because it's so expensive) honour of hosting it the following year. After winning in 1979, Israel passed on this 'honour' and, indeed, didn't participate at all in the 1980 contest because it coincided with the Jewish Passover. With Israel's absence, Morocco took part – without any success. There are now so many eligible countries that there is a preliminary competition to reduce the number.

Does a zebra sound like a horse?

We've been here before, haven't we? In *Why Eating Bogeys Is Good for You* (available in all good bookshops, etc.), I began my answer to the question *Why don't people ride zebras?* with the sentence: *Just because it looks like a horse doesn't mean it is one!* The same applies to this question. Although it looks like a horse (albeit one wearing jim-jams), it really isn't one and so rather than neighing or whinnying like a horse, the zebra makes a sound like a yapping dog and it does that in gasps – a bit like a donkey but not as loud.

Why is the scoring of three goals in a football match or taking three wickets in succession called a hat trick?

The term was first used in cricket to describe the feat of a bowler taking three wickets with consecutive balls. It dates back to the mid-19th century when, according to *The Oxford English Dictionary*, H. H. Stephenson took three wickets in three balls for the all-England XI against the 22 of Hallam at the Hyde Park ground, Sheffield, in 1858. A collection was held for Stephenson and he was presented with a cap or hat bought with the proceeds.' There's a second possibility that ties in with this: when a professional cricketer (cricket was then divided into amateurs who weren't paid and professionals who were) did something extraordinary, a hat would be passed around the spectators for them to put some money in for the player.

The term spread to other sports – so a rugby player who scores three tries in a match is said to have achieved a hat trick – and also to non-sporting feats: if a singer wins a Brit Award three years in a row, they might be said to have 'got a hat trick'.

Why do Americans pronounce the word *lieutenant* differently from the way we do?

Actually, that question should be the other way round: why do *we* pronounce it differently?

That's because we Brits got it wrong and the Americans got it (more) right!

The word *lieutenant* derives from French, in which *lieu* means 'place', as in a position; and *tenant* meaning 'holding', as in 'holding a position' – on behalf of a superior officer (as befits the junior rank of a lieutenant).

We say 'left-tenant' while the Americans say 'loo-tenant'. Now ask yourself which sounds closer to the original word 'lieu-tenant' – bearing in mind that the French pronounce the word 'lieu' as lee-yer.

The reason why we pronounce it left-tenant goes back more than 500 years, when the letters 'u' and 'v' were interchangeable: liev-tenant was pronounced as lev-tenant and then, eventually, 'left-tenant'.

Nowadays, though, with the spread of American films and TV, many British people use the American – the *correct* – pronunciation.

OSCAR
DEUTSCH
ENTERTAINS
OUR
NATION
SHOWING TONITE
GONE WITH THE WIND

Was there a Mr Odeon who started the chain of Odeon cinemas?

No, there wasn't. In fact, the use of the word 'odeon' to describe a building in which entertainment takes place goes all the way back to Sparta in the seventh or sixth century BC. So when cinema owners were thinking of names for their cinemas, they often chose 'Odeon'. In 1928, Oscar Deutsch was one such owner and he named his new cinema the Odeon. It was to be the first of several Odeons and his publicists later claimed that the name of the cinemas was derived from his motto: Oscar Deutsch Entertains Our Nation. But other cinemas – in Italy and France – had already used the name Odeon, so he (and his publicists) were just taking advantage of his initials!

Why is the 'Black Country' so called?

The Black Country is a loosely-defined area of the West Midlands – to the north and west of Birmingham and to the south and east of Wolverhampton.

It got its name because of the pollution from the heavy industries that covered the local area in black soot. However, it's also possible that the name existed even before these industries came into being – simply because of the coal, which was so near the surface that the soil was very black.

Why are pools of water called puddles?

The word *puddle* comes from the words *puddel, podel* or *pothel,* which are in turn derived from the Old English word 'pudd', which meant a ditch. The amount of water doesn't seem to have much to do with it – it's more about the hole or dent in the ground than the watery or muddy contents.

In practical terms, we can define a puddle as a pool of water big enough to step in and make your feet wet, but too small to sail a boat on.

What's the difference between a pig and a hog – or isn't there one?

A pig is a hog but a hog is not (necessarily) a pig!

Let me explain. *Hog* is a generic or general name for ALL swine. So a pig is a hog but there are hogs – like boars – that aren't pigs.

There's a word to describe the confusion that often sets in with questions like this and that word is 'syllogism'.

For example, all humans have legs. Agreed? All dogs have legs. Yes, that's also true. So does that mean that all humans are dogs? Of course it doesn't! That's called a syllogism.

How long is a light-year?

The light-year is a measure of distance, not time. As such, it's the total distance that a

beam of light, moving in a straight line, travels in one year. As for light itself, that travels at a constant speed of 186,000 miles per second. To give you an idea of just how fast this is, a traveller moving at the speed of light would circumnavigate the world along the equator about seven times a second!

Why does cream go stiff when whipped?

Cream goes thick when it's whipped because it's being mixed with air. There's a network of fat droplets in the cream that captures the air bubbles, and this effectively doubles the cream's volume.

Why is dog poo sometimes white?

There are two reasons for this. Although dog poo – like human poo – is naturally brown, if a dog has a diet rich in bones then its poo will be white. This was much more common in the old days, when dog food as such didn't exist and dogs just ate leftovers – usually just bones (which, being mostly calcium, were white in colour). People would ask their butchers for the bones they were throwing

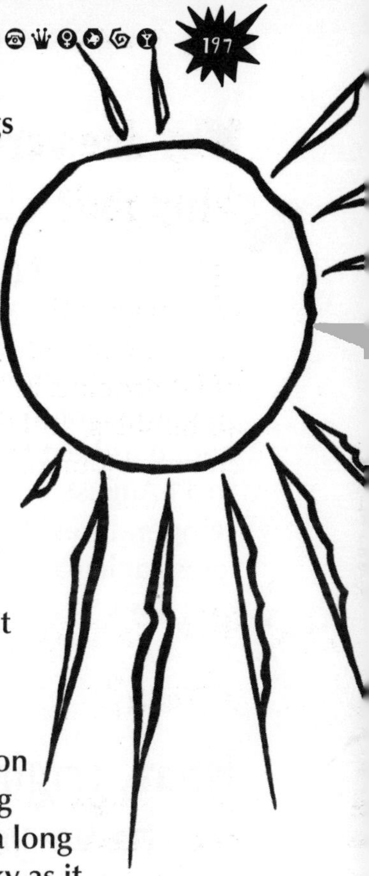

out to give them to their dogs – not as a treat (as we might do today) but for their basic food. Then manufactured dog foods came along. Early tins of dog food contained mashed bones in the form of 'bone-meal', but then came the BSE crisis and people became wary of having anything to do with the bones of dead animals in case they were infected, so bone-meal was no longer put in tins of dog food either. So dog poo became browner.

But there's also another reason for white dog poo. When dog poo has been in the sun for a long time, it turns white and chalky as it bleaches and dries out in the sun. Nowadays, however, owners are a lot more responsible and councils are far less tolerant of dog poo and so most of it is cleared up.

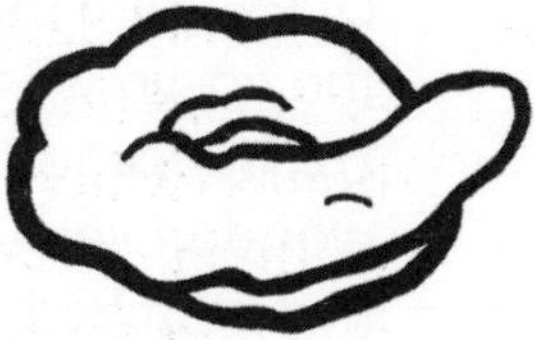

Why are very hot days called 'dog days'. Does it have anything to do with dogs?

No. This is a throwback to the Romans, who thought that Sirius, the Dog Star, added its heat to that of the sun from 3 July to 11 August, creating exceptionally high temperatures. The Romans called this period 'dies caniculares', or 'days of the dog' – hence dog days.

What, originally, was the point of the yo-yo?

Developed in the Philippines 2,000 years ago, the yo-yo was originally used as a weapon. For hundreds of years, warriors used square wooden versions covered with sharp edges and attached to thick long ropes. These were flung at human enemies or animals with, as you can imagine, devastating effect.

Over time, this weapon became a device to reduce stress and improve manual dexterity for soldiers until eventually it became a toy.

In 1929, the name 'yo-yo' was registered as a trademark by an American businessman named Donald Duncan, who went on to make his fortune from the popular playground toy. He had watched young Filipino children playing with home-made versions of the ancient weapons to cries of 'Yo-yo', which means 'come back' in Filipino.

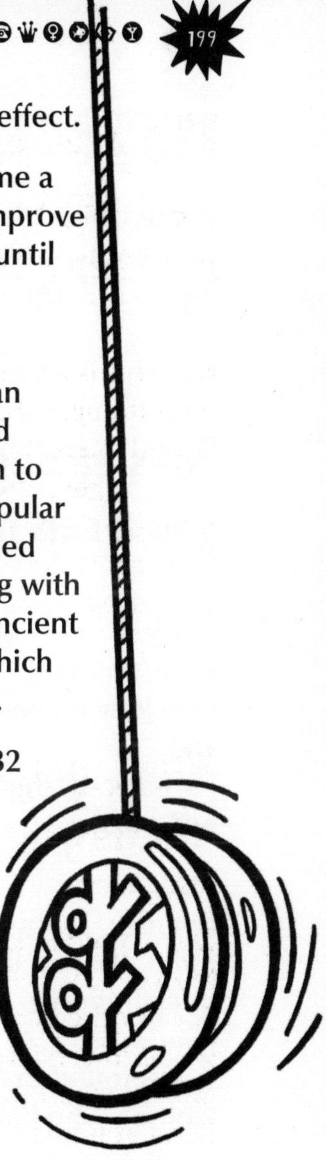

Yo-yos came to London in 1932 and were an instant success with – at the peak – weekly sales of 300,000. Everyone went yo-yo crazy. There have been periodic yo-yo crazes since then. These days, improved internal mechanics mean that even the ham-fisted can learn to perform impressive tricks such as 'walking the dog' and 'looping the loop'.

In the United States, there are not only shops devoted to selling yo-yos, but shops that exist just to sell replacement strings!

Does eating Jelly Babies make you a cannibal?

Gosh, I hope not as *love* Jelly Babies *and* I always eat them head first!

Also, in my defence, I should point out that in a scientifically-conducted test, it was found that women who had children of their own were more inclined to bite the Jelly Babies' heads off first; those who were childless tended to eat them whole.

So if mums can eat them head first then so can this dad!

Bassett's Jelly Babies were launched 75 years ago as 'Peace Babies', and were created by confectioner George Bassett to celebrate the end of the First World War.

The 'Peace Babies' were very popular during the inter-war period but production had to be stopped when the Second World War broke out because of a shortage of raw materials.

The popular little sweets reappeared after the post-war sweet rationing ended, in 1953. They were renamed Jelly Babies because of the time-lag.

Three million Jelly Babies are produced every week – more than a billion every year. Placed end to end, they'd stretch to New Zealand and back.

Although they are aimed at children, adult consumption of Jelly Babies is surprisingly high.

Why does vomit always contain carrots?

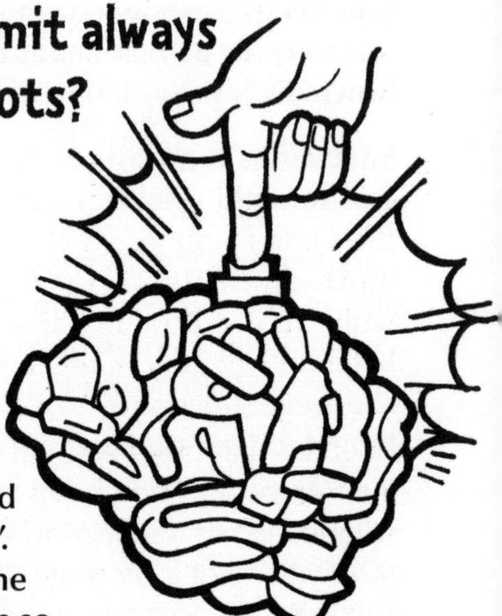

When something upsets your stomach and your body knows it has to get rid of it, a button is pushed in a part of your brain called 'the emetic centre'. This then rejects the stomach's contents so you vomit! The mushy, part-digested food or liquid in your stomach gets mixed with saliva or *spit* and acidic stomach juices (which give vomit its characteristic smell) and comes back up your throat and out of your mouth.

It is, as you probably know yourself, a ghastly experience.

So much so that there are lots of words in the English language to describe it – from emesis (the posh one), to puking, barfing, chucking up – even 'bowling it' for those who are forced to sit with their heads over the toilet bowl.

Sometimes it tastes like the food you just ate – or something a lot worse – and it's usually the same colour as what you last ate. Too much chocolate will look brown and yucky while an overdose of chips and tomato ketchup will look orange. Some foods like root vegetables and corn kernels take a lot longer for the stomach's acids to break down and digest, so even if you haven't just eaten carrots, swede or parsnips, they may be more noticeable than the more easily digested foods which have formed a general mush.

This is probably why vomit always seems to contain carrots – but it won't if you haven't eaten any.

One thing I can reassure you about: there's no truth to the rumour that the stuff-that-isn't-carrot-but-looks-like-it is part of the stomach wall lining brought up as a result of the violence done to the stomach through vomiting. It's just not true.

Historical note: Throughout the 17th and 18th centuries, there were many stories of people vomiting frogs and other amphibians. Several museums in Germany contained 'vomited amphibians' that had allegedly lived for years in a person's digestive tract. What a revolting thought . . . Fortunately, it's not true. We know now that the acid juices in your stomach would be much too powerful for anything to be able to live there, otherwise every time we swallowed a fly we would have fly eggs growing inside us.

The vomited amphibians were therefore a trick. For example, in 1834 a Mrs Henriette Pfenning appeared to vomit live frogs in front of applauding crowds of spectators. But she later admitted she'd been pretending and had hidden the frogs inside her skirt pockets.

Who performed the very first blood transfusion?

By the start of the 19th century, doctors and scientists had been trying to perform blood transfusions for well over a hundred years. In fact, the first human blood transfusion was attempted in 1668. They tried sheep's blood, but the experiment was unsuccessful and the patient died.

Then, in 1818, Dr James Blundell became the first person to try a human blood transfusion.

Blundell had seen too many women dying from loss of blood while giving birth and so he was determined to find a way of helping them.

Since doctors had already discovered that transferring blood from one species to another (i.e. animals to humans) not only didn't work but was positively harmful, Blundell knew that the blood for the transfusion would have to come from another human.

So he started a series of experiments using

animals and soon realized that a syringe would be the best way to collect the blood and then inject it into the patient. He also discovered the importance of letting all the air out of a syringe before a transfusion.

So one day, when Dr Blundell was treating a woman who had lost a lot of blood giving birth, he took some blood from the arm of her husband using a syringe, and successfully transfused it into the patient.

Thanks to this remarkable man, millions of people have lived who might otherwise have died. What a fantastic achievement – and yet I suspect his name is far less familiar than that of some silly wannabe celebrity who goes on a reality TV show. Funny old world, isn't it?

What is a wotsit?

A wotsit, or whatsit, is a thingamajig or a thingamabob. It's a word that we use when we can't think of the word we want.

Of course, it's most famous in its cheesy guise. Cheesy Wotsits were launched by Golden Wonder in 1971. The company used the name Wotsits as a working title for their new snack and it stuck because when the launch date arrived, nobody could think of a better name for them.

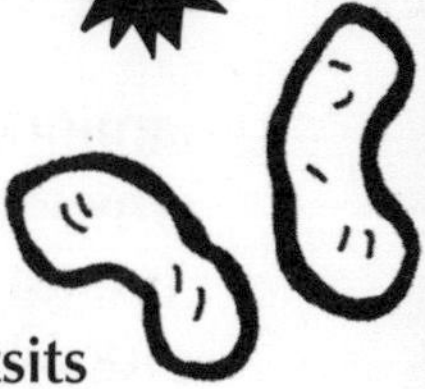

Is there more goodness in a potato's skin than in the potato itself?

There's no question that potato skins are very good for you as they contain fibre and keep the vitamins inside rather than letting them out into the water or air.

But it's not true to say that the skin has more goodness than the potato itself. Potatoes are also a great source of vitamins – including vitamin C and the vital B vitamins that help the body make healthy red blood cells and amino acids. Better than that, they don't have any fat in them – unless you fry them or add lots of butter. So it's wrong to claim that the outside is somehow better than the inside. The fact that potatoes are better with their jackets on shouldn't lead you to think that they're worthless without them.

Was Plasticine invented or discovered?

Plasticine was invented – not discovered – more than a century ago.

William Harbutt was an art school headmaster and teacher who used to visit the local schools in Bath to teach art. He was increasingly frustrated by the fact that the clay used by students for modelling was too hard and difficult to handle.

So he set about creating his own material and employed an old soldier to help him mix the ingredients and roll it out using a garden roller in the basement of his house. The water was squeezed out and rags were used to mop up the excess; the remaining modelling clay was then put through a fine dye plate and left to dry and mature for several weeks. It is said that there are still traces of Plasticine in the cracks in the floorboards of that house.

William's own children were allowed to play with the modelling clay and he realized that his invention had commercial potential: as a hobby for children as well as a teaching aid for budding artists. His earliest invention came only in battleship grey but he experimented to produce three colours – red, blue and yellow. The name of Plasticine was registered in 1898.

William and his family soon found themselves in business. At the start of the 20th century they bought an old flour mill in Bathhampton, near bath. When William's daughter Olive left school, she travelled around the country with him, demonstrating the versatility of Plasticine. Word spread, and soon they were selling Plasticine in the United States and around the world.

William died in 1921, having abandoned teaching in favour of trade. He was buried in the Bathhampton churchyard. His family continued the business.

Plasticine is very versatile and was used in the Second World War to make scale models of military defences and to draw up battle strategies. Winston Churchill played grim tactical games in Plasticine before issuing orders to his troops.

Plasticine is still an essential item in most school art departments. It is easy to use, doesn't crumble, get sticky or dry out, and keeps its shape after being moulded. Plasticine was given a big publicity boost

when Nick Park invented the characters of Wallace and Gromit, and their friends, who were all made out of Plasticine.

But although the Oscar-winning pair are famous all over the world, more astonishing still is the Plasticine City put together by two brothers, Martin and Nigel Langdon, in a remote Yorkshire vicarage.

They started building their city nearly 40 years ago when they were boys and had no money and no television. Using cocktail sticks as tools, they constructed a vast urban landscape, complete with a plaza, a Roman-style Coliseum and wide boulevards.

There are even skyscrapers, monuments and city parks.

For years they toiled in their separate bedrooms but then decided to amalgamate their efforts. They used up so much Plasticine that in the end, the manufacturers delivered the packs direct to their homes. William Harbutt would have been very thrilled to see their efforts.

Why is a two-piece swimming costume called a bikini?

In 1946, the island of Bikini in the Pacific Ocean was used by the Americans to test nuclear bombs. That same year, two French designers released their new two-piece swimming costume. Looking to cash in on all the interest in the nuclear tests, they claimed that their invention was so explosive that they were naming it after the site of those tests.

And so the bikini was born.

I guess it was lucky for them – and us – that the bomb tests didn't take place in the Sandwich Islands or else women would be going around wearing sandwiches . . .

What happens to the bullets that soldiers fire into the air to disperse crowds?

Before phoning Dr Adrian Newman, my pet physicist, I decided to do some research and was amazed to discover that people do indeed get killed when bullets are fired into the air even when it's just random shots fired in jest (which is why blanks are used for ceremonial purposes). Every year dozens of people die or are injured throughout the United States from stray bullets fired into the air during Independence Day and New Year's Eve celebrations. As Sergeant John Pasquariello of the Los Angeles Police Department, says, 'People that are shooting, they don't think they are out to kill anyone but they do.' Of course, it's a real problem in the States where anyone can own a gun (and anyone – or so it seems – does).

Now for the science. According to Dr Newman, 'When a bullet is fired vertically into the air, it immediately begins to slow down because of the effects of gravity and air drag on the bullet. The bullet deceleration continues until at some point the bullet momentarily stops and then begins to fall back towards earth. The bullet speed will then increase until it reaches its terminal velocity. The bullet reaches this when the air drag equals the pull of gravity – or, to put it another way, when the bullet weight and drag are balanced.'

I'm not entirely sure I understand.

'I'm not entirely surprised. Don't worry, it'll be easier when I introduce some figures into the explanation. A bullet fired into the air climbs two miles and remains in flight for more than a minute. As it falls, the bullet reaches a velocity of 300 to 700 feet per second. A velocity of only 200 feet per second is sufficient to penetrate the human skull. And that's why bullets fired into the air can – and do – cause deaths.'

Did Hitler ever come to Britain?

According to historian Dr Michael Morgan, there's every chance that he did. 'In 1973, Robert Payne wrote a book, *The Life and Death of Adolf Hitler,* that claimed he spent six months in Liverpool in 1912 when he was 23. At the time, Hitler was an impoverished art student and according to Payne, he stayed with his half-brother Alois and his wife Bridget at their home in 102 Upper Stanhope Street. Bridget – abandoned by Alois, who returned to Germany when Hitler took power – wrote her own book claiming that Adolf did indeed stay with them. It's hard to say either way: it certainly can't be disproved but most historians discount it as a rumour.

However, I can tell you that the Liverpool ice-rink keeps a pair of skating boots on display in a glass cabinet that were allegedly hired by Hitler.'

Why are comedies sometimes called farces?

All farces are comedies but not all comedies are farces. In other words, to use a mathematical expression, farces are a 'subset' of comedies.

Some comedies – although funny – are written to make serious points. That's not the case with farces: they're simply meant to make you laugh.

Farces derive their name from the Latin word meaning 'to stuff' because originally they were inserted as brief comic interludes in otherwise serious dramas.

Does the Loch Ness Monster exist?

Sorry to disappoint you, but almost certainly not!

The monster was first 'seen' in AD 565 by St Columba who saved the life of a man, being attacked by the monster.

Nothing more was heard about the monster until a newspaper article was published in 1933; a subsequent photograph – known as 'the surgeon's photo' because it was supposedly taken by a doctor – was released in 1934.

Then the world went Nessie (as the Loch Ness Monster was nicknamed) crazy. Loads of sightseers and holidaymakers went to Loch Ness – giving a much needed boost to the local tourist trade – and several people claimed to have made sightings of the creature.

Most were mistaken; the rest were being mischievous.

Eventually, with the advent of television and then, more recently, digital recorders, it became obvious that there was nothing there.

The final nail in Nessie's coffin came in 1994, when it was revealed that the surgeon's photo was, in fact, a fake.

What does the Brer in Brer Rabbit mean?

Simple question; simple answer. Brother.

Who invented Monopoly?

Monopoly was invented in America in 1933 by an unemployed heating engineer called Charles Darrow. He was inspired by a similar but dull game based on taxation.

His game was made up of bits and pieces collected around his home in Philadelphia. The board was made of linoleum; the houses and hotels were scraps of wood. He borrowed the charms from his wife's bracelet to make the players' tokens.

He and his family used to holiday in Atlantic City, so he based his hotel and street names on that resort.

The Darrows played their home-made game with friends, and it was so popular that Charles was asked to make copies for them. Soon he couldn't keep pace with demand, so he offered the idea to Parker Brothers, then the world's largest games maker. Their top executives sat down to play the game – and turned it down. Monopoly, they said, was far too complex; people would get fed up going round and round the board; and anyway it had '52 fundamental playing errors'.

Darrow set up on his own, making sets in his basement and selling them for $10 (then £2.50) each. Again they sold like hot cakes, and in 1935 Parker Bros made him an offer. They were soon selling 3,000 sets a day. Darrow became a millionaire and retired at the age of 46 to travel the world collecting orchids.

Monopoly was brought to Britain in 1935 by John Waddington Ltd of Leeds. The boss, Victor Watson, dispatched his secretary to London to collect place names for the British version. The Angel, Islington – the only pub named on the board – is where she enjoyed her lunch on her 'Monopoly tour'.

Very quickly, Monopoly became just as successful here as it had proved in the US. During the Second World War, the game took on an extra significance for British prisoners of war held by the Germans. They were sent special sets with tiny compasses and files, silk maps showing escape routes, and real local currency for use by escapers. For these players, 'Get out of jail free' wasn't just a card.

Monopoly is now made in braille for the blind and, thanks to American astronauts, has even been played in space.

Why are croissants the shape they are?

In 1686, some Hungarian bakers were working at night when they heard Turkish invaders digging underground to get into the city. The bakers alerted the people and the invaders were sent packing. To celebrate their part in the victory, the bakers created a pastry in the shape of a crescent (the Turkish emblem) and that's why the croissant is still crescent-shaped today.

What's the most common place name in the world?

San José. There are 1,716 – all named after St Joseph, patron saint of workers.

So if ever someone asks you (as in the song), 'Do you know the way to San José?' you're entitled to ask them, 'Which one?'

Are Scotch Eggs really Scottish?

No, they're not!

In fact, the eggs wrapped in sausage-meat, coated in breadcrumbs and then fried were first created in London by the prestigious food shop Fortnum & Mason, way back in 1738.

Why is 999 the number for the emergency services?

Good question. After all, back in the days when it was chosen, it would have taken longer to dial than any other number. I decided to ask social historian Penny

Chorlton (who also doubles as my wife). 'Until the 999 number was introduced, people were advised to phone Scotland Yard on Whitehall 1212. However, in November 1935 there was a London fire in which five people died. Part of the problem for the fire brigade was that the switchboard was jammed with well-meaning callers. So it became clear that a system was needed to distinguish emergency calls from all other calls. After much discussion between the Home Office, the Police and the Post Office, 999 was chosen because it was easy to remember and because it couldn't be dialled by mistake. It was also relatively simple to convert coin boxes to accept 999 calls without charge. The 999 system started in London in July 1937, and burglar Thomas Duffy was the first person to be arrested as a result.'

Why are soldiers called privates?

A private is a soldier of the lowest military rank. This goes all the way back to the Middle Ages, when privates – or private soldiers as they were known – were hired or forced into service by local noblemen who had been ordered to form an army for the monarch.

The reason why they were called private soldiers was because they were only responsible for themselves – unlike their officers, who performed *public* duty by being in charge of other soldiers.

Is the Caesar salad named after Julius Caesar?

No, it's not – although a lot of people think it is (hence the question!).

In fact, the Caesar salad – comprising lettuce (ideally romaine lettuce), croutons, Parmesan cheese and a dressing containing lemon juice, olive oil, Worcestershire sauce and anchovies – was invented by an Italian-born Mexican chef named Caesar Cardini in or around 1924.

Why is a replacement sometimes called a second string?

The expression 'second string', meaning 'replacement or backup', comes from the Middle Ages. An archer always carried a second string in case the one on his bow broke.

Why do we get electric shocks from car door handles?

Is there anything worse? I can't think of anything. I really, *really* hate static electricity shocks – the sort you get from car door handles and also (I don't know if it only happens to me) from metal hotel door knobs?

What causes it? And, much more important, what can we do to avoid it?

According to my friendly engineer, 'When you reach for a door handle – say on a car – and get an electric shock, it's only the release of electrical energy.'

But where does that come from?

'It develops because of the movement you made prior to touching the handle. There's a kind of mechanical interaction between your clothing and, say, the seat material of the car. To stop this happening, you should try changing your clothes as some materials attract more static electricity than others. Also, try to avoid sliding off the seat when you get out of the car.'

But what if I still get shocks?

'Two choices: you could try smacking the door handle . . .'

Really?

'Yes. Although you don't like static shocks, they're actually not very strong. What you hate is not the pain but the shock. Smacking the door handle . . .'

Even if it's done nothing wrong?

'. . . even if it's done nothing wrong – would hurt you more than the shock but at least you wouldn't really experience the shock because it would have been absorbed by the smack."

And the other choice?

'Stop being such a wimp, Mitch!'

And what about hotel room door handles? I asked, ignoring his unkind accusation.

'Same thing applies. Hotels often have synthetic – say, nylon – carpets and you can acquire quite a charge. Give the door handle a smack and that'll absorb the shock. Alternatively, you really could try to be a bit braver: even if you get them often, shocks from static electricity aren't dangerous. What are you worried about – that you might turn into a superhero or something?'

If I did, I know the first person I'd use my superpowers on . . .

What's the connection between Halloween and trick-or-treating?

This has its origins in a ninth-century custom called 'souling'. On All Souls' Eve (1 November), beggars would walk from village to village, begging for 'soul cakes'.

The villagers would give the beggars these cakes on the understanding that they would say prayers on behalf of the villagers' dead relatives on All Souls' Day (2 November).

This practice – minus the prayers and with the twist of the trick for the uncooperative – eventually became part of the ritual of Halloween.

Why is the pirate flag known as the Jolly Roger?

The Jolly Roger was actually the name given to *any* pirate flag. So although the most famous pirate flag is the skull and two crossed bones on a black background, the Jolly Roger is any one of several flags that pirates used to identify themselves. Even scarier – for other ships – than the skull and crossbones (as it came to be known) was the red flag, which indicated that the crew would fight to the death.

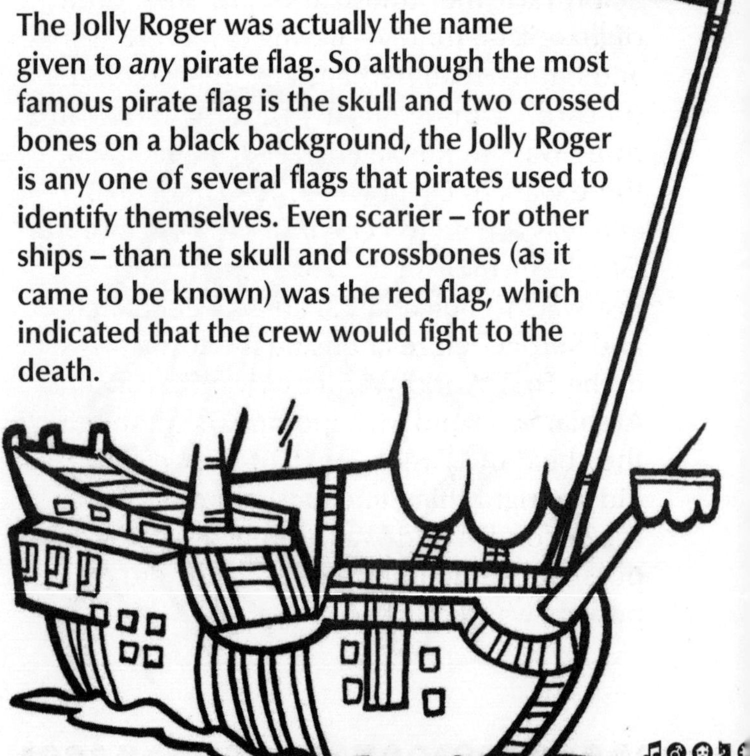

Which, when it comes to fighting wars, is the least successful country in the world?

It's hard to say for certain but, historically at any rate, the Turkish army has been a bit of a, well, er, turkey – having lost more wars and battles than perhaps any other nation on earth. During the 19th century, Turkey lost three wars to Russia (1812, 1829 and 1878), three wars to Egypt (1832, 1839 and 1840), and was forced to cede independence to the Greeks in 1827. In the 20th century, Turkey lost wars to Bulgaria, Albania, Greece, Italy and Serbia before choosing the losing side in the First World War (in which they lost Arabia, Syria and Mesopotamia). Although they beat the Greeks in 1922, they clearly did the right thing in choosing neutrality in the Second World War (though it is entirely possible that neither the Allies nor the Axis powers wanted them).

How did *The Guinness Book of Records* start?

It started – as so many things do – with an argument. It was 1951 and the boss of Guinness was out shooting when he got into a debate about the fastest game bird.

Refusing to let it rest, he contacted the McWhirter twins, Ross and Norris, who were well known as fact-checkers, and four years later, *The Guinness Book of Records* was born.

Now called *Guinness World Records*, it's been an annual bestseller ever since.

When was Britain's first National Lottery?

Britain's – or, rather, England's – first National Lottery was launched in 1567, to pay for public works. There were 400,000 tickets at 10 shillings each (though these could be subdivided 'for the convenience of the poorer classes'). The top prize was £5,000, of which £3,000 was paid in cash, £700 in plate and the rest in good tapestry, etc.

Why does someone who's trying to get attention get accused of 'stealing the limelight'?

Limelight – which originated in the burning of lime to create a strong light – was used by lighthouses and Victorian theatres before the era of electric light.

So someone who was trying to steal or hog the limelight was thrusting themselves into the middle of the stage at the expense of the other actors.

How fast can a car go in reverse?

Theoretically, you should be able to go as fast backwards as you can go forwards. After all, the engine runs at the same speed whether you are going forwards or backwards. However – and this is crucial – a car has gears and these enable a car to go faster or slower. So while a car will typically have four or five gears to go forward, it will only have one to go back and this will be the lowest gear (i.e. the equivalent of first gear).

The same is true of automatic cars, although with those, there's a little man sitting under the bonnet selecting the gears for you (that's how I've always understood it: please don't write in to correct me).

Incidentally, I'm assured by my mechanic friend that driving in reverse doesn't make the car's mileage go backwards.
What a pity!

Why do we describe something unfashionable as 'old hat' rather than, say, old jumper or old shoe?

Something is described as old hat if it's out of date or boring. The reason for this is because women's hats went out of fashion – i.e. became 'old hat' – long before they were past their best.

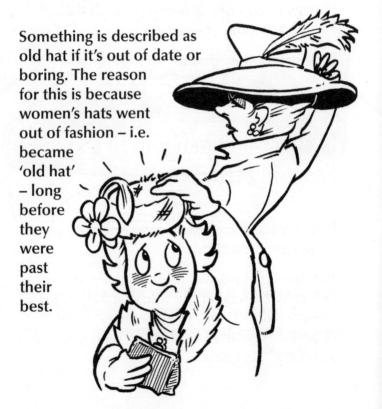

Why are earwigs called earwigs?

The word 'earwig' comes from the mistaken belief (or 'old wives' tale') that earwigs burrow into people's brains through their ears and then lay their eggs.

Fortunately, they don't!

Is there any penguin in a Penguin biscuit?

Penguin Biscuits were launched more than 75 years ago as Bluebirds.

The first Bluebirds were made by the biscuit maker McDonald in the Tollcross bakery in Glasgow in 1933 and the layered crunchy chocolate biscuit in its cheerful wrapper was an immediate success.

The name was changed to Penguin in the 1940s but, like most luxury foods, went out of production for the duration of the war. Biscuit manufacturers were called on by the government to make iron-fortified plain biscuits instead, chocolate being in very limited supply.

After rationing ended, the biscuits were advertised in newspapers and magazines by penguin characters. When TV advertising was introduced, real penguins were employed to sell the product. In the 1960s, Derek Nimmo borrowed his stuttering curate character from the popular television series *All Gas and Gaitors*. The 'P-p-p-p-p-pick up a P-P-P-P-Penguin slogan he popularised became part of the English language.

The earliest biscuits came in milk chocolate flavour only, but nowadays you can buy a dark chocolate variety and also Penguin cakes, as well as sub-brands like Penguin Chukkas, Wing Dings, Flipper Dipper, Splatz and Mini Splatz. Although there is still a McVitie's bakery in Glasgow, Penguins are no longer made there, having migrated to Manchester in the 1970s (McVitie, like

McDonald, was bought by United Biscuits and became the producer of Penguin biscuits). These days, technology has moved into the bakery, with computers prescribing the exact quantities needed to make each batch. The whole operation from weighing the ingredients to wrapping them in red, blue, yellow or green, takes 45 minutes. During this time, the biscuits move on a conveyor belt through a 100 metre-long oven, cooling on the way. Technical developments have also made it possible to make the penguins who advertise the biscuits on television appear to talk.

Oh, I nearly forgot to answer the question. Is there any penguin in a Penguin? Well, what do you think? They are, after all, suitable for vegetarians . . .

Is that really the sound of the sea we hear when we put a shell to our ear?

It would be nice to think it was but, alas, it isn't. Instead, what you're hearing when you put a shell (or, indeed, a cup or a glass) to your ear is the blood flowing through your head.

The reason why people thought they were hearing the sea is because the shape of the shell makes an excellent echo chamber. Also, the wish is father to the thought: the noise from the shell sounds like the sea because your brain is processing the sound and looking for something it has heard before that makes sense now: perfectly reasonably, it connects the sound with the object being held to the ear – in this case the *sea*shell.

We sail boats and fly planes – so how should we describe what we do to submarines?

On the surface of the water, you steer a submarine or even sail it but when it's submerged, you would say that you're 'driving' it.

Why do we dream?

In common with nearly every other mammal, we dream while we sleep. Dreaming helps our brains grow – which is why newborn babies dream about eight hours a day. Dreams also serve the purpose of filtering our thoughts to help us solve problems.

By the way, don't think that just because you don't remember your dreams that you're not having any: many of us don't remember them and most of us dream in black-and-white.

Is there an explanation for the nursery rhyme that starts 'Seesaw Marjorie Daw'?

Seesaw Marjorie Daw
Johnny shall have a new master
He shall earn but a penny a day
Because he can't work any faster.

You've probably sung this on a seesaw yourself. I've looked into this and I think that Marjorie Daw is just a name used to make the rhyme work. But the stuff about Johnny having a new master and earning but a penny a day is a chilling reference to child labour. Workhouse children were made to work in exchange for bed and board but were paid appallingly.

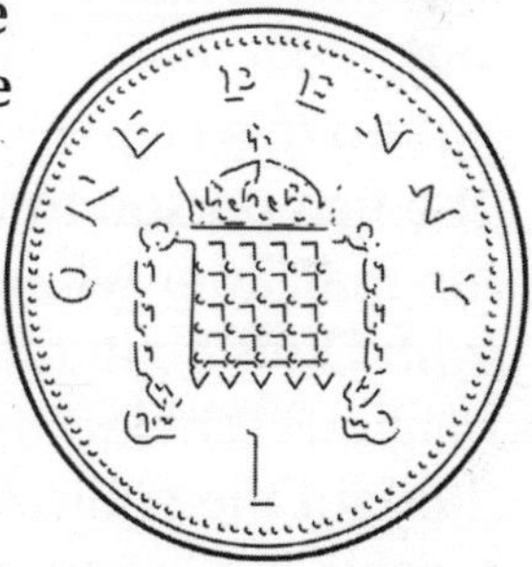

Who was the first person to wear a dunce's cap?

In days gone by, children who misbehaved at school would be put in the corner and made to wear a cone-shaped dunce's cap. Some cruel teachers would even send the pupil who came last in a test into the corner and make them put on this cap.
The first person to wear the dunce's cap was the man after whom it was actually named: John Duns Scotus, an Oxford theologian (or religious scholar) of the 14th century who thought the conical hat would help him receive messages from God.

Fast forward a couple of centuries and philosophers were sneering at John Duns Scotus and his followers – known as Dunses or, later, Dunces. They were, it was believed, stupid and incapable of learning. And so the conical-shaped dunce's cap became associated with stupidity and, eventually, bad behaviour.

Luckily we don't have the dunce's cap in schools these days!

Why does someone who's in trouble have to 'face the music'?

Although there are other possible explanations for this saying, the one I like best goes back to the days when army court-martials (or, as these trials of soldiers should technically be known in the plural, 'courts-martial' – which simply sounds wrong!) were even more formal than they are today.

As the commanding officer read out the

charges against the soldier to be tried, an army drummer would drum by his side.

The soldier on trial would therefore be 'facing the music'.

So if a soldier – or later, as the saying became more widely used, a civilian – was going to be doing something risky or even illegal, he would talk about 'facing the music' if he was caught.

Interestingly, another expression is associated with this one. If someone is 'fitted up' – i.e. accused of doing something bad that they didn't do – then they would be facing 'drummed-up' charges or the case could be described as 'drummed up'.

How essential is an orchestral conductor?

When they have a classical concert, there's always a person (usually a man) standing on a podium facing the orchestra telling them what to do. In one hand he has a stick – known as a baton – which he uses to point at different sections of the orchestra. He uses the other hand to control the beat or tempo of the music.

Some conductors become incredibly famous and wealthy (the conductor is almost always the best paid of all the performers in a concert).

But how vital is he?

What would happen if he didn't turn up?

Would the concert have to be cancelled?

I have a friend who plays the violin in an orchestra so I asked him what he thought.

'The first thing you have to understand is that a conductor doesn't just turn up on the day and fling his arms around. His job is more like that of a theatre director: he rehearses the orchestra and gives his interpretation of a piece of music.'

So what would happen if he didn't turn up on the day?

'That depends on how well he'd rehearsed and prepared his musicians. They'd probably be all right if they'd really worked hard at it for long enough, but then we'd still end up taking our lead from the orchestral leader, who is, as you know, the lead violinist.

'Of course, if it was a piece of music that we

knew really well and had played several times before then it really wouldn't matter if the conductor were absent.'

Would the audience see the difference?

'I doubt it: a real music fan might notice slight differences – perhaps in timing. What the rest of the audience would really miss is the passion and the energy that a really great conductor brings to his work.'

When did
the lollipop lady
first start helping
children to cross
the road?

In 1953 there was a lot of concern about the increasing levels of traffic and the danger to children walking to and from school. So the government introduced the School Crossing Patrol Service. Because of their distinctive 'lollipop' paddles, they soon became known as lollipop ladies and men.

The first school crossing patrol began working on the busy London streets in the summer of 1953. By the winter, every local authority in the country was trying to sign up its own team of part-timers for duty every school day, 8 a.m. to 9 a.m. and 3 p.m. to 4 p.m.

Within a year, there were more than 1,000 men and women putting themselves at risk to protect school-aged children from oncoming traffic.

Countless lives have been saved by these brave individuals who go out in all weathers to stop the traffic and let children cross safely. Many patrols also help with road safety and awareness lessons in the schools they serve.

A high proportion of patrollers have first aid training, and further training is currently underway to allow patrols to play their part in child protection. There is a special fluorescent uniform consisting of a longish yellow plastic raincoat and a peaked black cap.

Recently, there has been a shortage of lollipop people throughout the country as it is not seen as a very glamorous job, the pay is poor and it takes a lot of commitment.

As well as increasing traffic, another hazard is drivers with road rage. In 1999, Derby City Council was the first authority to run special courses in dealing with such drivers. Three of their wardens had needed hospital treatment after being hit by cars, and more than 60 complained of intimidation by drivers. The lollipop people were given special training originally used to help nightclub bouncers deal with drunken clubbers.

There are 30,000 lollipop men and women in Britain employed by the local authorities. Together, they have done a remarkable job in keeping down the number of children killed on our roads. Child deaths in road accidents have declined sharply since their introduction, despite the massive increase in traffic.

So the next time a lollipop person enables you to cross the road safely, thank them.

Is Cluedo a British or an American game?

Nowadays, the detective board game Cluedo is truly international, with more than three million sets sold around the world in more than a dozen different languages, but it started off in Britain.

Cluedo was invented by Anthony Pratt, a Midlands-based solicitor's clerk, in 1944. Anthony and his wife Marjorie were enthusiastic 'gamesters' whose favourite activity was playing board games with their friends.

It was Marjorie who designed the board itself, as the fictitious home of the victim, Dr

Black. For three years they played their home-made 'Cluedo' among friends before they were urged to submit it to Waddingtons, the Leeds-based games manufacturer, for possible commercial mass-production.

The company liked the game immediately, and knowing that thrillers and anything to do with crime always appealed to the public imagination, launched it officially in 1948.

The game was so successful that the Cluedo characters of Miss Scarlett, Colonel Mustard, Professor Plum and so on have become household names in the last 50 years. Indeed, there was national outrage when Waddingtons announced in 1992 that they planned to de-frock the Reverend Green and make him plain old 'Mr' – as he is known in many of the 23 countries where the game is sold.

For anyone who doesn't know, or has forgotten, the rules, Cluedo takes place at a country house where six guests are gathered, and six weapons concealed. There are nine rooms, including a conservatory, library and billiard room, and the purpose of the game is to discover who, when and where – but never why – poor old Dr Black met his grisly end.

There are 324 potential murder combinations, which perhaps explains why it is a game that can be played repeatedly without players tiring of it.

By the way, just for the record, it was Mrs White in the Kitchen with the Rope.

Why doesn't the mountain K2 have a name instead of a number?

K2 stands in the Karakoram range of the Himalayas between Pakistan and China. However, climbers have to go there via Pakistan as the Chinese side is inaccessible. It is called K2 because it was the second peak of the Karakoram range (there were four other mountains in that range), according to the European team that first surveyed the range in 1856. However, since then, other countries have given the mountain names – for example, it's known as Lamba Pahar (or 'Tall Mountain') in Urdu. But its default name has always been K2.

It's the world's second highest peak (after Mount Everest) at 8,611 metres above sea level, and was first scaled in July 1954 by two Italian climbers, Lino Lacedelli and Achille Compagnoni.

Why does a doctor who becomes a specialist have to change his title to 'Mr'?

Yes, that does seem unfair! They train for all those years in order to earn the right to call themselves doctors – then, after becoming surgeons, they have to change back to Mr or Mrs, which anyone is allowed to use without having done a single day's medical training.

I checked with a surgeon I know and he told me that he was extremely proud to become a 'mister' and assured me that he still used his doctor title whenever it suited him or if there was any doubt about his profession.

The reason for the distinction goes back to the days when medicine and surgery were entirely separate professions. Medical people – or physicians as they were known – went to university or medical school and became doctors. Surgeons, on the other hand, were considered to be master artisans – like carpenters or silversmiths – and were trained on the job as apprentices to qualified surgeons. Consequently, they weren't doctors but, like any other artisans or tradesmen, misters.

Nowadays, all surgeons have to undergo the same medical training as physicians (doctors who aren't surgeons) so they're called doctors until they become surgeons, whereupon they will be known as misters. Unless they're female, in which case they're known as Mrs, Miss or Ms.

Was there a real Jack Sprat?

Jack Sprat could eat no fat
His wife could eat no lean
And so betwixt the two of them
They licked the platter clean.

Sounds like an ideal marriage, doesn't it? The husband likes his meat without any fat (understandable) while his wife only likes eating fat (less understandable). No need to order two meals at a restaurant and, what with the clean plate, they're going to save on washing-up liquid when they eat at home.

In fact, like so many nursery rhymes, this was less innocent than it sounds. Far from being a

simple poem, it was mocking the monarch of the day, King Charles I, who'd become 'lean' because Parliament had refused to finance his war against Spain. Meanwhile his wife, Henrietta Maria of France was accused of getting 'fat' at the people's expense.

Why, traditionally, do husbands carry their wives across the threshold?

This is an old tradition – and yet it's surprising just how many men still carry their wives or girlfriends across the threshold (i.e. through the front door) of every home they live in, the day they first move in. And why do they do it? Well, in the old days it was done to protect them from being possessed by evil spirits that hang around in doorways.

Nowadays, it's done as a romantic gesture!

Why is it pink for girls and blue for boys?

This is something I really don't get. What does it matter? They're only colours! And yet I know otherwise intelligent people – parents-to-be – who wouldn't decorate the new baby's bedroom before it was born because, since they didn't know its gender, they didn't know what colour paint to use.

How crazy is that?

At least there was a reason for the original thinking of having separate colours. Since all babies look pretty alike with their baby clothes on, it was decided to identify their gender through the use of different colours. It started in ancient China, where, as in many cultures, baby boys were considered more valuable than baby girls (traditionally, when the boys eventually married, their family would receive a gift of money, in the form of a dowry, from the bride's family).

In those days, pink dye was readily available and therefore inexpensive. But blue dyes were rare and difficult to make, so this colour was reserved for sons to emphasize their greater value!

In ancient times it was believed that evil spirits threatened the well-being of infants and the colour blue was thought to ward them off – but people didn't want to waste any of the valuable blue dye on girls so they stayed in pink.

These traditions persisted through the ages until the present day and that's why it's pink for a girl and blue for a boy – even though nowadays it's nothing to do with a child's 'value' and everything to do with the idea that pink is more feminine while blue is more masculine.

Interestingly though, this is not as widespread as you might think and there are other cultures and countries (Belgium, for example) where it's actually the other way round: many people dress baby boys in pink and baby girls in blue.

What do the letters BMW stand for?

The car company BMW, which was founded in 1916, stands for 'Bayerische Motoren Werke'. Fortunately for them, when translated into English, that becomes Bavarian Motor Works – which means that they can keep the same initials!

Why is it that fish served in a restaurant is always accompanied by a slice of lemon?

It's partly because lemon goes so well with fish but also because of a strange belief dating all the way back to the Middle Ages. It was thought that if a person accidentally swallowed a fish bone, the juice of a lemon would dissolve it.

Where did the teddy bear originate?

This is a tricky one because both Germany and the United States claim to have invented the teddy bear at about the same time – in 1902.

The teddy bear almost certainly owes his name to Theodore (nicknamed 'Teddy') Roosevelt, who became President of the United States in 1901. While visiting the Southern States he went off on a bear hunting expedition, one of his favourite sports. His hosts, embarrassed by their failure to flush out any real bears, captured and tethered a small black bear cub as an easy target. His refusal to shoot the defenceless animal became the subject of a newspaper cartoon and there was a huge sympathetic response from the American public.

Morris Michtom, a Russian immigrant, kept a shop selling sweets, novelties and stationery in New York. He suggested that his wife Rose, a skilled toy and doll-maker, should make a soft toy bear out of plush fur-like material. Her finished bear was put in the window alongside a copy of the famous cartoon with the label 'Teddy's Bear'

Morris Michtom got President Roosevelt's permission to use his nickname but, alas, the letter giving this permission was lost, and with it the absolute proof that the teddy was an American invention! No matter, the wholesalers, Butler Brothers, bought Michtom's entire stock of bears, setting up the Ideal Novelty and Toy Company in 1903, and became one of the most successful American toy businesses.

Meanwhile in Germany, there was a rival claim to the invention of the world's best-loved toy.

In the 1880s, seamstress Margarete Steiff, who was crippled by polio as a child and confined to a wheelchair, worked from home making soft animal toys from felt. In 1889 she opened a toy shop. Her nephew Richard gave her designs for a stuffed plush bear, based on his drawings of bear cubs in Stuttgart Zoo. In 1902, she made the hump-backed bear, stuffed with wood shavings; it had jointed limbs and life-like movements similar to a doll's. It was shown at the Leipzig Toy Fair in March 1903, but was not an instant success, remaining neglected until towards the end of the fair, when an order for 3,000 was made – in part because of the strength of the bear craze that was raging in the United States. The small Steiff family business expanded dramatically to cope with the American demand for teddy bears. Margarete herself was said to be stunned by the reaction.

The number of bears produced by the firm rose from some 12,000 in 1903 to an amazing 974, 000 in 1907.

Teddy bear mania reached its peak during Roosevelt's second term of office, 1905–1909. It was in 1906 that the description 'Teddy's bear' soon shortened to 'teddy bear'. Britain became the second biggest importer of Steiff bears. The teddy bear's famous furry coat was made from 'plush', a fabric woven from mohair yarn, which was spun with angora goat wool.

German teddies were banned in Britain during both world wars, giving rise to British-made bears. Chad Valley made their first bear in 1915, as did Chiltern Toy Works, whose Master Teddy was dressed in check shirt and patched felt trousers with braces. Daphne Milne bought one from Harrods in 1916 for the first birthday of her son, Christopher Robin; with the name Winnie-the-Pooh, it went on to become the central figure of her husband A. A. Milne's stories.

So is the teddy bear American or German in origin?

I think we can say with some certainty that it's American but that the Germans perfected it (Steiff teddy bears are still the most valuable and go for several thousands of pounds when they come up for auction), and were responsible for introducing the teddy bear into Britain and Europe.

Is it possible to improve your memory?

Yes, it is. But first, you must understand that the brain is just like any other part of the body: it requires use and practice. So here are some things you can do to improve your mind and memory:

- As soon as you wake up, write down your dreams . . . if you can remember them.

- Do sums in your head. Start with single digits and then move on to double digits.

Keep a dictionary near you so you can look up words you don't understand, and then practise using your new words – try a new one every day if you can, as a sort of game with yourself. This is the easiest way to extend your vocabulary.

Put a collection of objects in a bowl or on a tray and study them for about a minute. Then close your eyes and try to remember what was there. Repeat until there is no difference between what you see and what you can remember.

Retrace in your mind a recent journey (it doesn't matter if it was on foot, by car or on a bus or train). Try to remember as much about it as you can – the sights, the sounds and even the smells . . .

Learn to listen twice as much as you talk – you will learn more if you are not 'jammed on transmit'.

Have at least 10 minutes complete silence each day – if necessary go for a walk or sit on a bench. This gives your mind time to think . . .

Learn a new board game or card game every week . . . especially games like Scrabble or chess that require you to think, rather than those that just rely on luck – though Snap tests your reflexes. Practise with your friends and relatives to sharpen your wits.

Improving your balance also helps: try holding one leg up by the foot and balancing on the other . . . then do it again swapping feet. When you can do this without wobbling and falling over, try doing it again, but this time with your eyes closed. If you find it hard, ask your mum or dad to try it. That should make you feel smarter already!

Who invented the kaleidoscope – and did he make a fortune from it?

The world divides into people who collect things and people who don't. My wife collects lots of things (enamel boxes, for example) whereas I don't collect anything – although that's not to say that I don't seem to have an awful lot of rubbish in my office!

Anyway, I've often thought that if I were to collect something, it would be kaleidoscopes. I love them and find them endlessly fascinating.

As I'm sure you know, a kaleidoscope is a tube-shaped optical instrument that you twist to produce a succession of symmetrical designs. These are created by mirrors reflecting the constantly changing patterns made by bits of coloured glass at the end of the tube.

It was invented by an extraordinary man named Sir David Brewster in 1817. And he named it after the Greek words meaning 'observer of beautiful forms'.

Let me tell you about Sir David, a child prodigy who built his first telescope at the age of 10. At 12, he went to university.

He was one of the most eminent physicists of his period, and he left behind an intriguing set of scientific instruments. He would have been astonished to know that of all his many inventions, his most lasting would be something regarded by most people as a children's toy.

Brewster was fascinated by light and how it could polarize and form shadows and reflections and he devoted his life to studying it. The invention of the kaleidoscope came out of these studies but he didn't think it would become a toy: in fact, he thought it might be useful for designing carpets!

Alas for him and his family – when he applied for a patent (to protect his invention), he didn't fill out the forms properly and so other people were able to manufacture kaleidoscopes and make money from them.

He went on to design a novel optical system for lighthouses (in 1835) and was involved in the early development of photography. He also developed the stereoscope, a device that by using two lenses and two pictures taken from slightly different perspectives, provides an illusion of 3D. The resulting toy, the red plastic Viewmaster, sold very well.

Sir David himself never made any money out of his inventions, although he was showered with scientific awards for his academic work and was knighted. All his life, he was terrified of speaking in public.

Nevertheless, in spite of himself, he became something of a celebrity and had quite a few famous friends – including the author Sir Walter Scott. By the standards of the day he lived a long life, dying in Melrose, Scotland, in 1868 at the age of 87.

Is it true that the sirloin steak was so called because it was knighted by a monarch?

It's a great story and one that a great number of people actually believe but it simply isn't true!

According to the legend, King Henry VIII (though I've heard it ascribed to other kings too) was so impressed by a particular cut of meat that he decided to knight it. 'Arise, Sir Loin.'

Well, what do you think?

No, I don't believe it either. So what's the truth?

A lot more boring, I'm afraid. The cut of beef or steak known as 'sirloin' comes from the (old) French word *surlong* – meaning 'above the loin'. Surlong became 'surloin' and, eventually, 'sirloin'.

Where was chess first played?

The game originated in ancient India (as 'Caturanga') – although the word 'chess' is derived from the Persian word 'shah' (meaning king or ruler). By the 10th century AD, chess was played in most European countries.

Does a car's air conditioning use up more fuel than having the windows open?

Yes, it does. However, on a hot day it might be more fuel efficient to have it on rather than to leave the windows open.

Obviously, the speed at which the wind drag caused by having the windows open uses up more fuel than the air conditioning is going to vary from car to car. But, basically, at below 50 mph, it's more fuel efficient to leave your windows down; over 50 mph, it's more fuel efficient to put on the air conditioning.

Given that hedgehogs have hard spikes, does a female get injured when she gives birth?

Fortunately for hedgehogs – well, mother hedgehogs anyway – baby hedgehogs are born with very soft spikes. Almost as soon as they're born, these spikes harden to provide protection for the baby hedgehog or hoglet.

Who invented candyfloss?

Candyfloss is simply ordinary white sugar which is dropped into a specially designed machine and spun at very high speed. The heat forms thin strands which, when wound round a stick, form the fluffy ball that we all know and love. The pink colouring is added separately. Other colours are possible, merely by changing the colour of the dye.

Candyfloss was invented in 1897 by William Morrison and John Wharton, who were sweet manufacturers in Nashville, Tennessee. Together, they developed a machine that allowed crystallized sugar to be poured onto a heated spinning plate.

They proudly took their 'Fairy Floss' to the 1904 St Louis World's Fair, a showcase for new inventions where the world's first ice cream was launched. It was a huge success and they sold 68,655 Fairy Floss machines. Among their early customers was Thomas Patton, a vendor at the Ringling Brothers and later the Barnum & Bailey Circus. For many years he was erroneously thought to be the inventor of candyfloss.

Novel though the idea was, the early machines could be very temperamental, often breaking down and losing income for the vendors who operated them. In 1949, the spring-loaded base was invented by the Gold Medal Products Company of Cincinnati, which still makes most of the world's candyfloss machines.

The candy in candyfloss (or cotton candy as it is known in the US) is derived from the

Persian word 'Kandisefid', which means white sugar.

Candyfloss is still known as Fairy Floss in Australia, while in other parts of the world it is known variously as *suickerspin, barbe à papa, algodón de azúcar* and *zuccero filato*.

Candyfloss is hugely profitable and has been likened to a cash machine for its owners, promising 90% profit on overheads. Despite its name and image, candy floss contains fewer calories and less sugar than a can of cola.

What's the difference between a turtle and a tortoise?

Along with terrapins, turtles and tortoises belong to the same family: testudines.

All testudines look pretty similar – having shells on their backs. However, whereas the tortoise, with its larger domed shell and thicker, stockier legs, is well adapted to living on land (only approaching water to drink or bathe), the turtle has a flatter shell and thinner legs, making it more streamlined for swimming.

Why is something very hot described as 'piping' hot?

Before electric kettles, we had steam kettles. The way you knew they'd boiled was when the steam set off a whistle. Another (naval) term for a whistle is a pipe. From water to anything else, piping soon became the word to describe great heat.

There's another naval tie-in with this expression. In the Royal Navy, orders are 'piped'. If you came to dinner as soon as the order was piped, then the food would indeed be piping hot.

Why does my nose run?

There are several different reasons why your nose might run.

If you have a cold or flu, your body makes lots of mucus to keep germs out of your lungs and the rest of your body. All the hairs in your airways also work to get bacteria and dirt out of your lungs and into your mucus. The mucus then runs down your throat, out of your nose, or into a tissue when you blow your nose. Often it runs into your head – which is why you get that horrible stuffy feeling and a funny voice when you have a cold.

People with allergies also get runny noses when they're around the thing they're allergic to (like pollen or animal hair). That's because their bodies react to these things as if they're germs.

Your nose also runs when you cry because when tears come out of the tear ducts in your eyelids, they don't just run out of your eyes but also into the large open space behind your nose called the nasal cavity. The tears run down your nasal cavity and into your nose, where they mix with the mucus and pour out.

Your nose may also run when you're playing outside on a cold day. This is because the air in your nose is much warmer than the outside air (which is also why you can see your breath) and the warm water drops mix with your mucus, and run out of your nose.

How long did the Hundred Years War last?

You'd think the answer would be a hundred years. The clue is, after all, in the question. And wouldn't you feel stupid if this question came up at a quiz and you gave the wrong answer – only to discover that it was a trick question and the answer was indeed a hundred years?

Well, I suppose it *is* a trick question because the answer isn't a hundred years. Technically speaking, it actually lasted *longer* than a hundred years – 116 years in fact – and it wasn't one long war like the First or Second World Wars, but a series of wars between England and France.

The first one started in 1337 and the last one ended in 1453 – which is why I said it lasted 116 years. However, there were many brief interludes and two lengthy periods of peace, so in reality the fighting took place over 81 years. The two countries were fighting for the throne of France. There were two contenders: the House of Valois (a French dynasty) and the House of Plantagenet, which was then ruling England (in those days, England and France frequently shared monarchs and, besides, the Plantagenets had their roots in France).

The war – dubbed the Hundred Years War by historians much later – eventually ended in 1453 with the defeat of the Plantagenets.

Did the Black Death affect any other country apart from Britain?

The Black Death was the most deadly pandemic in history – killing 75 million people in the 14th century.

And that should give a clue to the answer to the question: the population of Britain – even before the Black Death – was a tiny percentage of the total number of people killed.

No, the Black Death (or the Black Plague as it was also known) started in Asia and spread to Europe by the late 1340s, where it killed up to half of all the inhabitiants.

Whole villages were wiped out and in some places the dead outnumbered the living. You can imagine the terror of the few who survived the badly hit towns and villages. The Plague – also known as the Bubonic Plague – returned to England in the 17th century, but fortunately fewer people died.

Little prawns are always sold peeled (without their shells). Does this mean that people have sat there peeling them for us?

No, don't be silly! The prawns are scooped up from the sea in gigantic trawlers and are put through no fewer than four machines to peel them. The first machine is like a huge rolling pin that squeezes the prawns gently so that they pop out of their skins; another machine blows away the shells; and further machines using lasers inspect the prawns for any remaining bits of shell. The only part of the process involving real people is the final one where the prawns are inspected for quality.

Prawns can be divided into cold-water and warm-water types. Cold-water prawns live on the muddy bottom of the sea. The prawns you find in your sandwich or prawn cocktail are the small cold-water prawns.

The bigger prawns – also known as tiger prawns – come from warm waters. They're not just more expensive than the little prawns on a per-prawn basis (which is fair enough); they're also a lot more expensive by weight (i.e. per 100 g), which seems most unfair but perhaps reflects how much harder they are to catch.

Bizarre but true fact: prawns spend the early part of their life cycle as males and the latter part as females.

What's the difference between a first, a second and a third cousin?

This is something that's always confused me and, if I'm honest (and I always am – honestly!), I didn't really find out the truth till I researched this question.

Growing up, I'd hear someone described as a second cousin or a third cousin or, even more confusingly, a second cousin once removed.

All very puzzling. So let's try to make some sense of it.

Let's start with the easiest: first cousins. If your mum or dad have brothers or sisters, then *their* children are your first cousins. In other words, first cousins are people who share a set of grandparents.

If you've got that, then let's move on to second cousins (if you haven't got that, then I urge you to stop reading now because it really does start to get complicated!). Your second cousin is the son or daughter of one of your parents' first cousins. In other words, second cousins are people who share a set of great-grandparents.

As for third cousins, they're the children of your parents' second cousins – and here you share a set of great-great-grandparents. You can carry on doing this until you get to 20th (and beyond) cousins. But it's silly. If you carry on long enough, you'll find that you're related to everyone in the world – which ultimately, I suppose, you are! Beyond third cousin, it's best to use the expression 'distant cousins'. Here are some examples of distant cousins: Madonna and Gwen Stefani; Tony Blair and the Queen; Oprah Winfrey and Elvis Presley; John Grisham and Bill Clinton.

Now for this wretched word 'removed'. What's the difference between, say, a first cousin and a first cousin once removed? The answer is surprisingly simple and can be expressed in a single word: generations. It's still a question of sharing ancestors, but they're from different generations. So, for example, my mother's first cousin and she have a grandmother and a grandfather in common: they 'share' them. But what relation am I to my mother's first cousin? The answer is first cousin once removed. Her grandmother and my great-grandmother were the same person.

If you can understand that (and millions of people can't), then you might see that my mother's first cousin once removed (that's to say a generation above her) would be my first cousin twice removed (that's to say two generations above me) and that this relative and I would share an ancestor who is their grandparent but my great-great-grandparent.

There's a lot of fun to be had with cousins once you start 'removing' them (so to speak) because that's when you can find yourself related to fascinating people in history. For example, when Diana, Princess of Wales, the late mother of Princes William and Harry, married Prince Charles, people explored her 'family tree' and discovered that she was related to some extraordinary folk.

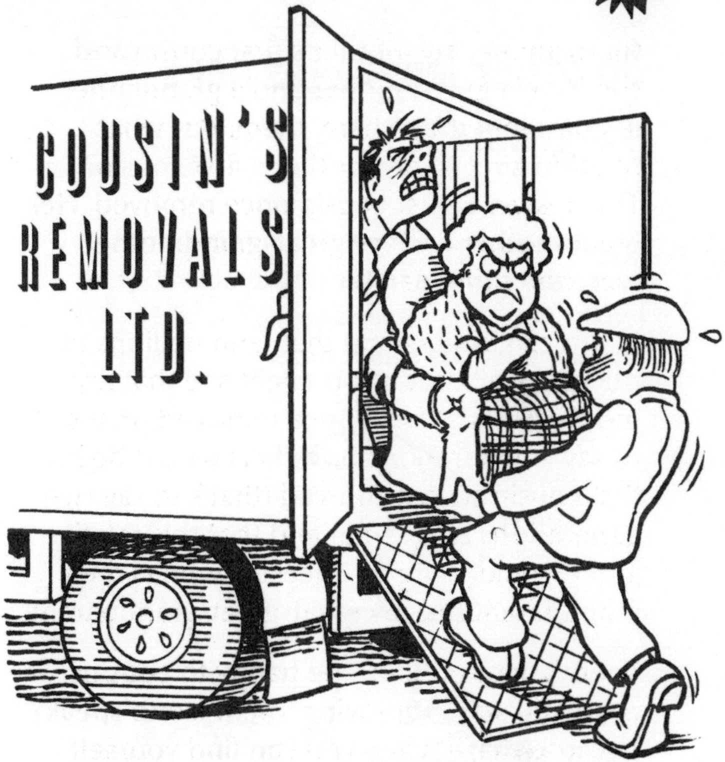

For example, she was Sir Winston Churchill's fourth cousin twice removed; the author of *Little Women* Louisa May Alcott's seventh cousin four times removed; Oliver Cromwell's first cousin eleven times removed; and Jane Austen's seventh cousin six times removed.

Do other languages have pangrams?

A pangram is a phrase or sentence that uses every single letter of the alphabet at least once. The most famous in the English language is 'The quick brown fox jumps over the lazy dog.'

That at least means something and – because this is the point of pangrams – in remarkably few letters (35 – try to work out which letters are used twice). Here are other pangrams which are certainly brief but possibly just a little harder to understand:

Bright vixens jump; dozy fowl quack.

Waltz, bad nymph, for quick jigs vex!

Junk MTV quiz graced by fox whelps.

The shortest I could find (without using proper nouns, abbreviations or acronyms) was just 27 letters: *Big fjords vex quick waltz nymph.*

Can you make up a meaningful sentence using all 26 letters of the alphabet?

However, pangrams aren't just fascinating games to play with letters and words: they also have a use. Because they use every letter of the alphabet, they're ideal for testing printers or (in the old days) typewriters.

That's why several other languages also use them.

Here are some examples:

Dutch: *Pa's wijze lynx bezag vroom het fikse aquaduct* (meaning: Dad's wise lynx piously observed the sturdy aqueduct).

French: *Portez ce vieux whisky au juge blond qui fume* (meaning: take this old whisky to the blond judge who's smoking).

German: *Franz jagt im komplett verwahrlosten Taxi quer durch Bayern* (meaning: Franz chases in the completely unkempt taxi straight through Bavaria).

Was the Slinky invented as a toy or did it ever have a practical use?

During the Second World War, an engineer in the United States Navy named Richard James was on a new ship. He had been trying to invent a spring that could help keep sensitive nautical instruments balanced while on rough seas. By accident, he knocked some of these experimental springs off a shelf, and was fascinated by the way they 'walked down', rather than just falling.

When Richard James returned home, he remembered the springs and their interesting movements and made one to show his wife, Betty. She was entranced and so they decided to make it into a toy.

He spent the next two years figuring out the best steel gauge and coil to use in making the toy while Betty came up with a name for it: 'Slinky' – a Swedish word meaning sleek or sinuous.

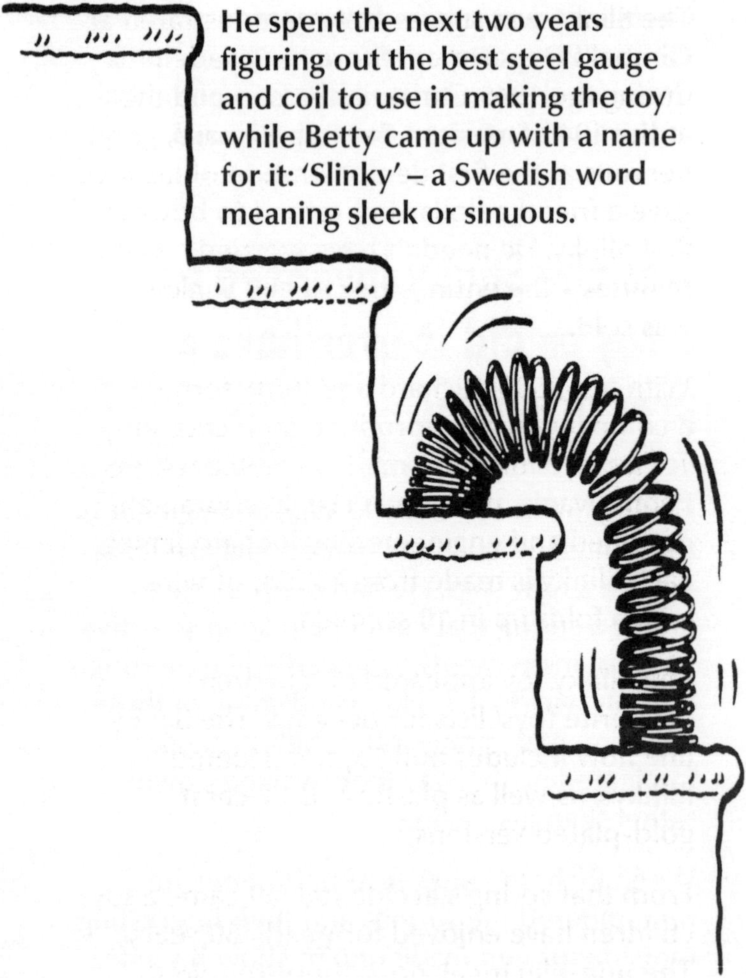

The Slinky was successfully demonstrated at Gimbel's Department Store in Philadelphia during the 1945 Christmas season and then at the 1946 American Toy Fair. Richard, very nervous at the first demonstration of his toy, gave a friend a dollar to pretend to buy the first Slinky. He needn't have worried – within minutes – the entire stock of 400 Slinkys was sold.

With just $500, Richard and Betty formed a company to mass produce their creation. Today, all Slinkys are made in Hollidaysburg, Pennsylvania, using the original equipment designed and engineered by Richard James. Each Slinky is made from 80 feet of wire which folds up in 10 seconds.

The Slinky toy appeared on children's 'favourite toys' lists for decades. The Slinky line now includes pull-toys, 'costumed' Slinkys, as well as plastic and 14-carat gold-plated versions.

From that spring's accidental fall came a toy children have enjoyed for nearly 60 years. The non-electrical, no-battery-required, non-video toy has fascinated three generations of children and adults alike. The metal Slinky is different from the original only in that the sharp ends are crimped for safety. It was judged by *The Toy Book* to be one of the top 10 toys ever invented. There are slinky dogs and Slinky Pets as well as one called Crazy Eyes, which has slinky extended fake eyeballs!

More than 300 million have been sold worldwide and in excess of 50,000 tons of wire have been used since the Slinky first went into production. If you joined them all up, they would encircle the earth more than 126 times.

Why is table tennis sometimes called Ping-Pong?

I always thought that they were precisely the same thing but that

Ping-Pong was a slightly silly expression used to make table tennis sound more like a game than a sport.

In fact, I was wrong: although Ping-Pong is a game, it started life as a superior version of table tennis – thanks to the quality of the equipment used.

So that's it: the difference between Ping-Pong and table tennis is that table tennis is the game whereas Ping-Pong is a trademark version of it.

In fact, the name Ping-Pong was in wide use before the British manufacturer J. Jaques & Son Ltd trademarked it in 1901. It then came to be used for the game played by the rather expensive Jaques equipment, with other manufacturers calling theirs table tennis.

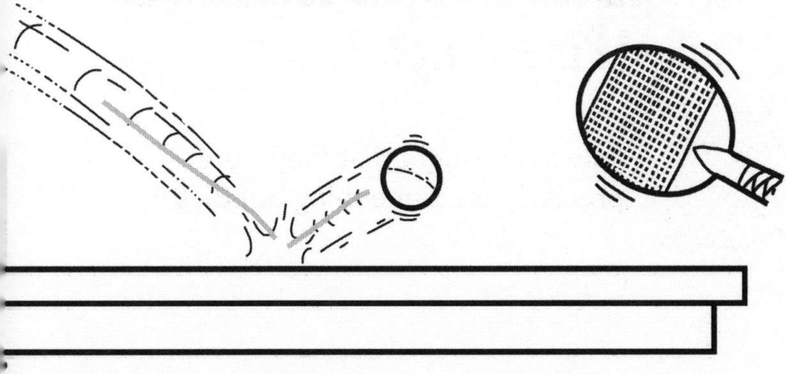

Jaques then sold the rights to the name and the equipment to companies in other countries.

I suppose it's a bit like cricket also being known as, say, 'Tip and run' and some company coming along and trademarking 'Tip and run' in order to sell cricket equipment under that name. The games would still be the same, it's just that one – cricket – would be available to everyone (what's called 'generic') while the other would be a trademarked game with its merchandising rights protected by law.

See also the vacuum cleaner (generic) and the Hoover (trademarked) or sticky tape (generic) and Sellotape (trademarked).

Is it true that you can see the Great Wall of China from outer space?

Sadly, no, you can't (although when I write 'sadly', I don't think too many of you will be going to outer space to find out for yourselves).

It turns out it was an urban myth that originated in a *Ripley's Believe It Or Not* cartoon in 1932. This was repeated in many books since, including some school textbooks.

Not surprisingly, no lunar astronaut has ever claimed they could see the Great Wall from the moon.

Mind you, the Great Wall is such an extraordinary structure that you can see why people were able to believe this myth.

It is a series of fortifications built over several centuries between the 5th century BC and the 16th century. It is some 6,700 kilometres long

and it has been estimated that up to three million people died during its construction.

These days, the wall is in a sorry state of repair, though the parts near the tourist centres have been preserved and even reconstructed. Elsewhere, some sections are used as village playgrounds and many of the bricks and stones have been used to build houses. Some have been vandalized, while others have been destroyed because the wall is in the way of proposed roads. Nobody has

attempted a comprehensive survey of the wall so it's not possible to say how much of it survives, especially in the more hilly and remote areas.

It is inconceivable that such a massive feat of engineeering will ever happen again, though perhaps the building of artificial islands like The Palm and The World in Dubai are the modern equivalents of man altering the physical landscape.

Is it really possible to charm a snake?

Snake charming is the practice of apparently hypnotizing a deadly snake simply by playing an instrument. It is common in North Africa, especially Egypt.

I always thought it was a total con but it seems there is something to it!

The snake charmer usually sits cross-legged on the ground in front of a closed pot or basket. He takes off the lid, and starts playing a flute-like instrument made from a gourd – a type of vegetable. As if drawn by the tune, a snake emerges from the container and begins swaying to and fro in time with the musician's tune, apparently hypnotized. If it's a cobra, it may even extend its hood. The snake never strikes, and the charmer may sometimes kiss the normally fierce creature on the head, as if to show how the music has entranced and dulled its normal aggression.

Astonished onlookers throw coins and notes

to the successful performer. When it looks as if the crowd's generosity has been exhausted, the snake returns to its container and the charmer replaces the lid and gathers up his earnings.

The truth is that standing erect and extending the hood is a normal defensive reaction for a cobra. The snake is reacting to losing its cosy dark environment, where its blood temperature was low, making it feel groggy.

The snake's swaying movement is actually a reaction to the movement of the performer's instrument, or sometimes the tapping of his foot. Snakes are actually deaf, though they can feel vibrations. While it can't hear the tune being played, it can perhaps feel the vibrations as well as the tapping of the charmer.

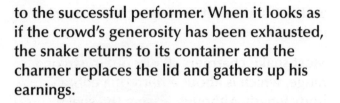

The snake's apparent reluctance to attack is because – contrary to what you might think – most snakes prefer to scare off possible predators rather than fight them; they are generally quite timid, unless they're attacked. It returns to its basket because the snake charmer stops his waving motion and not because it is obeying its 'master's' instructions.

Most snake charmers sit just out of striking range, which is about a third of a cobra's body length. Although kissing the snake might seem to be tempting fate, it's actually not very risky as cobras are incapable of attacking things above them – though don't try this if ever you come across one! Though some claim that snake charmers drug the snakes to sedate them, this is rare.

Interestingly, although snake charming is mostly done as a tourist spectacle, in some parts of the world it is done to sell snakebite *remedies* – to people in countries like India, Pakistan, Malaysia, Sri Lanka, Thailand, Egypt, Morocco and Tunisia, where snakes are a genuine hazard.

There is only one native venomous snake in Britain – the adder – though others have been released as ex-pets that have grown too big. The last death from an adder bite in the UK was more than 30 years ago, but adders do bite people if they come across them walking through areas of long grass or heath land . . .

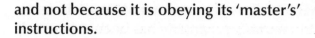

which is why it's a good idea to wear long socks and boots rather than sandals!

More people die of snakebites in India than in the rest of the world's countries put together. A variety of poisonous snakes kill 50,000 Indians a year.

And yet most of these deaths are preventable. In Australia, where there are even more more venomous snakes, deaths are so rare they make headlines. So your chances of getting bitten by a snake are highest in Australia but that is where most of the research is being done on antidotes so you've got a good chance of being saved.

Some countries don't have any snakes – places like Ireland, Greenland, Iceland and New Zealand. It's thought this is because they are surrounded by water . . . but then so are many other islands, which do have snakes!

By the way, here's a story I came across in the course of my research. If you don't like snakes, don't read it!

In 2002, a butcher living in Bandar, east of Dhaka in Bangladesh, heard a mysterious noise underneath his floorboards. He called in veteran snake charmer Dudu Miah and his assistants from a neighbouring village.

They dug up more than 3,000 poisonous cobras below his sitting room. Neighbours fled in panic as the full scale of the catch became apparent.

'This is the largest stockpile of snakes I've ever found in my life,' said Mr Miah, the snake charmer, who later ate at least a dozen of his catches.

Why is an ice-cream cornet with a Flake in it called a 99?

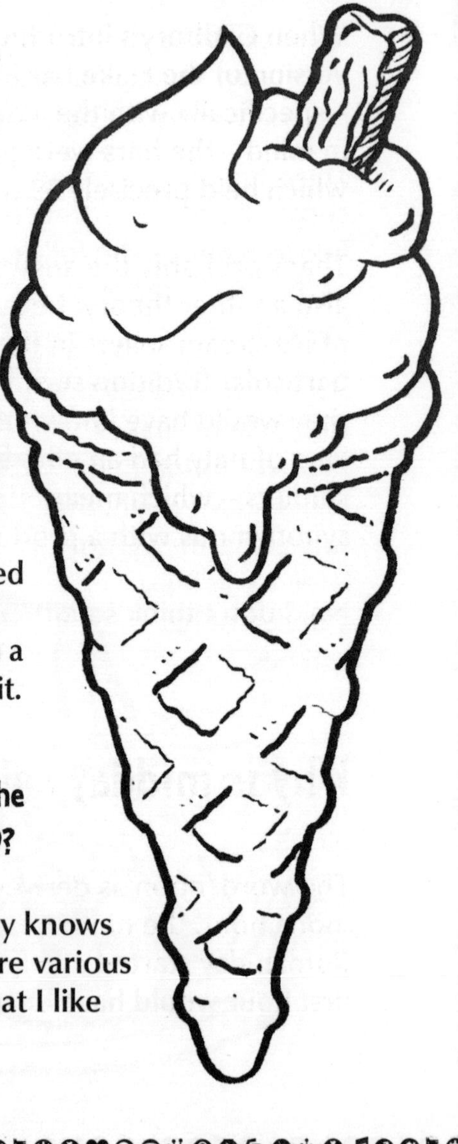

There's nothing like soft vanilla ice cream in a cornet from an ice-cream van – especially one covered in chopped nuts and chocolate sauce with a Flake sticking out of it. Pure heaven!

But why does adding the Flake turn it into a 99?

It seems that nobody knows for sure, but there are various theories. The two that I like the best are these:

When Cadbury's introduced the smaller version of the Flake bar in the 1930s – specifically with the ice-cream van market in mind – the bars were packed into boxes which held precisely 99 of them.

That's probably the answer, but consider also another theory: because the majority of ice-cream sellers in the 1930s (when this particular tradition started) were Italian, they would have known that, historically, the king of Italy had an elite bodyguard of 99 soldiers – which meant that the number was synonymous with a product of high quality

No, I don't think so either!

Why is midday called 'noon'?

The word 'noon' is derived from the Latin 'nona hora', the ninth hour of the day. As the Roman day started at 6 a.m., at sunrise, the first hour would have been from 6 till 7 a.m and the ninth hour from 2 till 3 p.m. These hours were particularly important in monasteries, as different prayers were held at different times. So the English word 'noon' was originally applied to 3 p.m., but by AD 1100 the meaning had shifted to 'midday'.

And what caused this shift? No one knows for sure but I found this wonderful story that could explain it!

There was a monastic order (that's to say a group of monks in a monastery) so devout that they declared they wouldn't eat until 'nona hora' or 'none' (i.e. 3 p.m.). But the monks were – understandably – hungry, so they rang the bells for 'none' earlier and earlier. Eventually, the people in the town near the monastery teased them by calling midday 'noon'.

I don't know if it's true but it deserves to be!

Will a boomerang always come back?

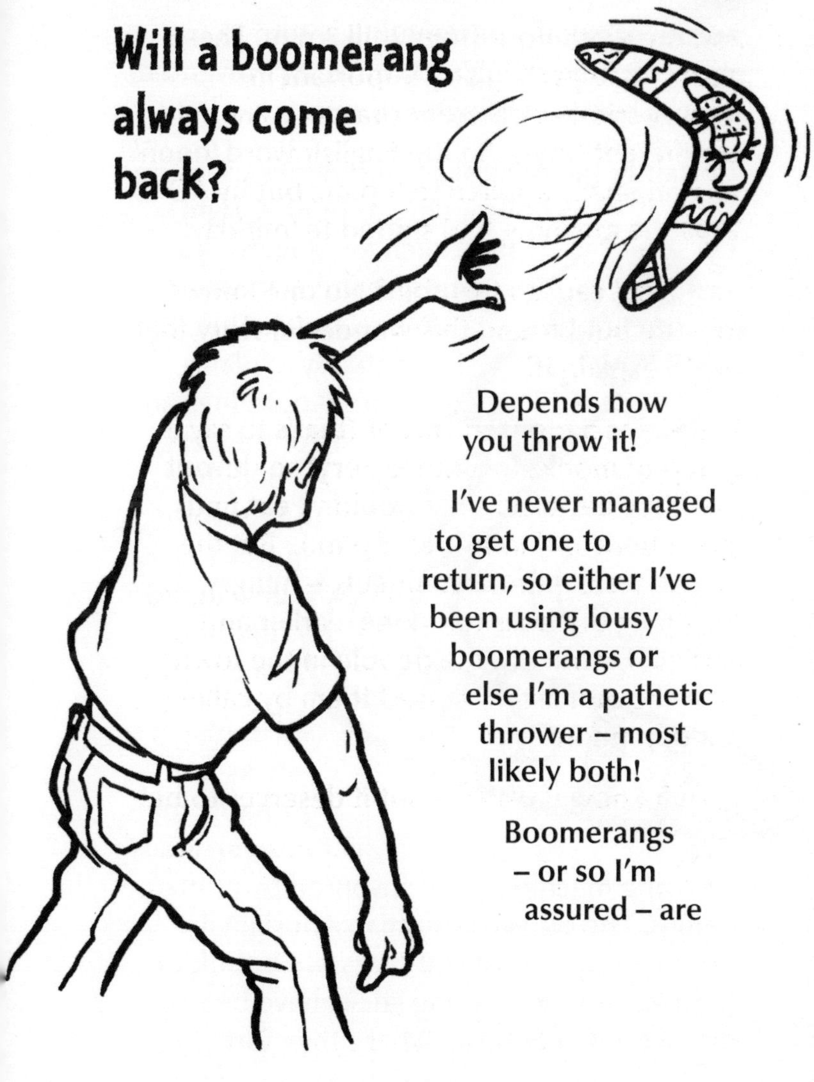

Depends how you throw it!

I've never managed to get one to return, so either I've been using lousy boomerangs or else I'm a pathetic thrower – most likely both!

Boomerangs – or so I'm assured – are

aerodynamically designed to return to the thrower; interestingly, they weren't invented as toys but as hunting weapons.

Certainly, the Australian Aborigines used the boomerang to hunt upright prey such as kangaroos and emus, roaming in vast open country. This probably explains why Aborigines are one of the very few peoples of the world never to have developed the bow and arrow.

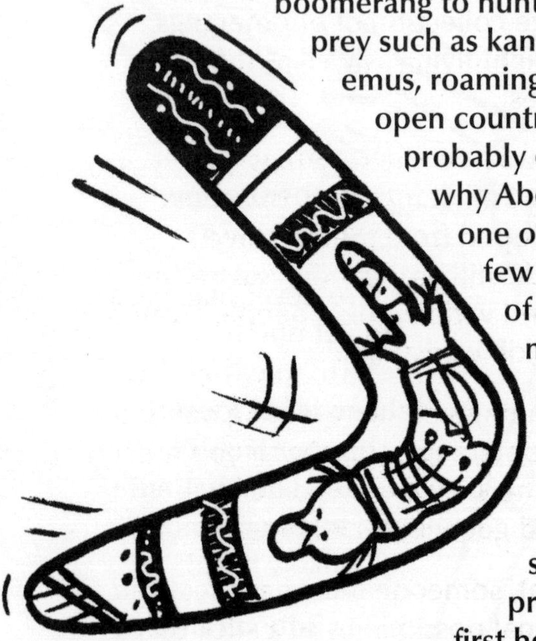

Hunting sticks are probably the first heavier-than-air flying machines ever invented by human beings. The oldest Australian Aboriginal boomerangs are 10,000 years old but older (non-returning) hunting sticks have been discovered in Europe, where they formed part of the Stone Age arsenal of weapons. Boomerangs were used in India as well as in the ancient Orient and in medieval Europe. King Tutankhamun, the famous pharaoh of ancient Egypt, who died 2,000 years ago, owned a huge collection of boomerangs, both the straight flying as well as the returning ones.

Nobody knows how the returning boomerang was first invented, but some think it developed from the flattened throwing stick, still used by the Australian Aborigines and various tribal people around the world to kill wild animals.

The real advantage of the returning hunting stick – or boomerang – was that if you missed your target, the stick would come back to you and you'd get another chance.

At some point, someone must have realized the recreational possibilities of a stick that comes back when you throw it away.

Or, in my case, not . . .

Why do flamingos stand on one leg?

Let's say you were outside on a very cold day and all you had on was a short-sleeved T-shirt. What would you do to keep your arms warm?

My guess is you'd hug them as close to your body as possible so as to keep in the heat.

Well, that is exactly what the flamingo does. By tucking one leg in close to its body, it's able to stay warmer in cooler weather.

But it's not just the cold the flamingo is trying to avoid – there's also the damp: flamingos spend a lot of time in water looking for food, so by changing legs they give the other one a chance to get dry.

It might look hard to us but it isn't to them. Flamingos (and many other birds) can stand on one leg for more than four hours at a time and never lose their balance.

But I'm sure there are things you can do that they can't!

Questions I wasn't able to answer . . .

Why is it that when two planes almost hit each other it's called a 'near miss' when it's really a 'near hit'?

How can a product be described as 'new and improved'? If it's new, it can't be an improvement.

Is clumsiness catching – or is it dropping?

What do sheep count when they can't get to sleep?

If many hands make light work, how come too many cooks spoil the broth?

If a mime artist is arrested, does he have the right to remain silent?

Why doesn't the word 'anagram' have an anagram?

How do you get rid of stain remover?

Why doesn't superglue stick to the inside of the tube?

How does the man who drives the snow plough get to work in the mornings?

Why is it called 'rush hour' when cars move so slowly?

If you tell a joke in the forest, but nobody laughs, was it a joke?

Why are there flotation devices under plane seats instead of parachutes?

Why do floorboards only creak at night?

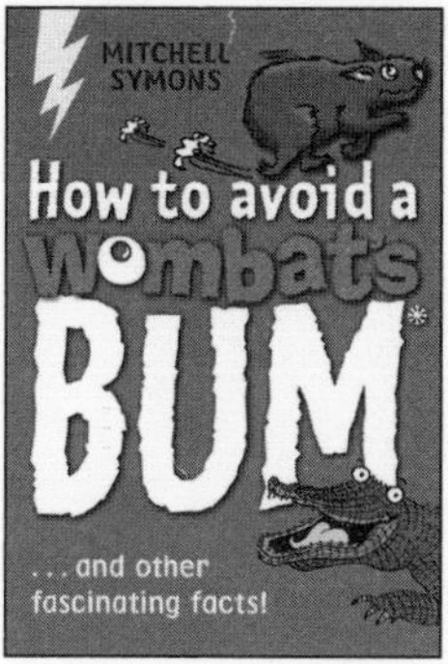

Mitchell Symons

HOW TO AVOID A WOMBAT'S BUM*

And other fascinating facts!

* Don't chase it! Wombats can run up to 25 miles per hour and stop dead in half a stride. They kill their predators this way – the predator runs into the wombat's bum-bone and smashes its face.

Amaze and intrigue your friends and family with more fantastic facts and figures:

- most dinosaurs were no bigger than chickens
- Everton was the first British football club to introduce a stripe down the side of players' shorts
- A snail has about 25,000 teeth
- No piece of paper can be folded in half more than seven times

Just opening this book will have you hooked for hours!

978 1 862 30183 2

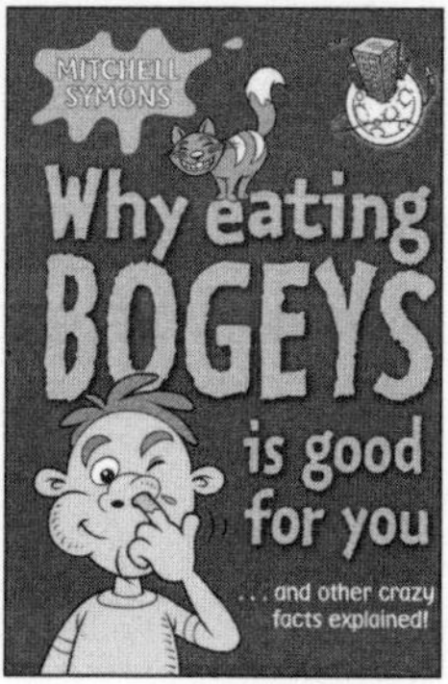

Mitchell Symons

WHY EATING BOGEYS IS GOOD FOR YOU

And other crazy facts explained!

Ever wondered . . .

- Why we have tonsils?
- Is there any cream in cream crackers?
- What's the best way to cure hiccups?
- And if kangaroos keep their babies in their pouches, what happens to all the poo?

Mitchell Symons answers all these wacky questions and plenty more in a wonderfully addictive book that will have you hooked for hours!

(And eating bogeys is good for you . . . but only your own!)

Selected for the booktrust Booked Up! Initiative in 2008.

978 1 862 30770 4

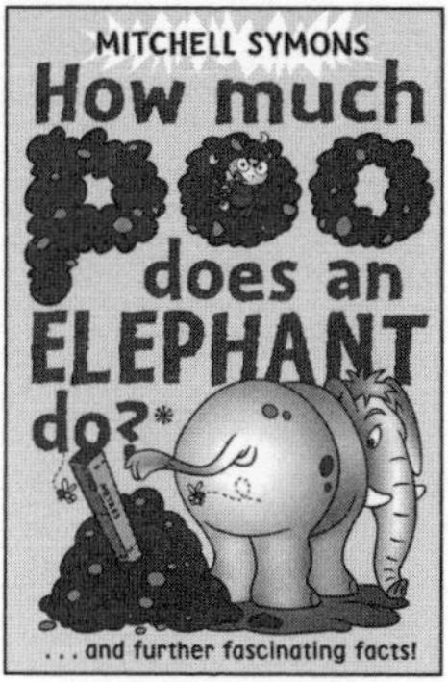

Mitchell Symons

HOW MUCH POO DOES AN ELEPHANT DO?*

And further fascinating facts!

* an elephant produces an eye-wateringly pongy 20 kilos of dung a day!

Let Mitchell Symons be your guide into the weird and wonderful world of trivia.

- Camels are born without humps
- Walt Disney, creator of Mickey Mouse, was scared of mice
- Only 30% of humans can flare their nostrils
- A group of twelve or more cows is called a flink

978 0 385 61365 1